EDITOR: LEE JOHNSON

OSPREY
MILITARY
MEN-AT~~~~~~~S 124

COMMANDERS
OF WORLD WAR II

Text by
ANTHONY KEMP
Colour plates by
ANGUS McBRIDE

First published in Great Britain in 1982 by
Osprey Publishing, Elms Court, Chapel Way,
Botley, Oxford OX2 9LP, United Kingdom.

ISBN 0 85045 433 6

Filmset in Great Britain
Printed through World Print Ltd, Hong Kong

FOR A CATALOGUE OF ALL BOOKS PUBLISHED BY
OSPREY MILITARY, AUTOMOTIVE AND AVIATION
PLEASE WRITE TO:

The Marketing Manager, Osprey Publishing,
PO Box 140, Wellingborough, Northants, NN8
4ZA, United Kingdom

or visit Osprey's website at:
http://www.osprey-publishing.co.uk

The German Armed Forces

This book contains brief outlines of the careers of a number of the senior German commanders during the Second World War. I have purposely chosen a representative selection of those who exercised considerable field commands, rather than those like Halder and Keitel who were purely staff officers. I would emphasise that the selection is my own and does not imply any order of priority or even merit.

To those who read military history many of the names are familiar. It is a paradox, however, that few biographies have been written except in the case of 'pop' generals like Rommel. The impression still exists today of German generals as stiff-necked, scar-faced, monocled Prussians. In a few cases this was certainly true, but the fact remains that all of them were men, some more ordinary than others. No army had a monopoly of competence; and the German armed forces, even if they produced only one or two soldiers who will go down in history as 'great', had a large number who will be found worthy of the second rank.

Owing to limitations of space it is impossible to discuss the development of the German officer corps at length, but it is important to grasp a certain amount of the background in order to be able to understand the actors on the stage of war. Hitler was fond of saying that he had a Christian Navy, a reactionary Army and a National Socialist Air Force, which was to a large extent true.

In Germany the Army had always been the senior service and had a long history of involvement in politics. This remained indirectly the

Two studies of Generalfeldmarschall Wilhelm Keitel – a confident studio portrait showing him at the pinnacle of his fame as head of OKW (Armed Forces High Command); and a Russian photograph of his signing of the instrument of surrender in 1945. Keitel, who owed his position to his marriage to von Blomberg's daughter, was an unintelligent and characterless yes-man who acted as the conduit between Hitler and his generals; respected by nobody, he survived throughout the war simply by virtue of dog-like loyalty to a master who described him as having 'the brains of a cinema usher'. Among professional colleagues he was known as 'Nickeitel' or 'Lackeitel' – 'nodding' or 'lackey' Keitel. His signature was found on many damning documents, and he was hanged for war crimes on 16 October 1945. (Imperial War Museum, and Novosti)

case after the end of the First World War. The Treaty of Versailles reduced the Army to a cadre of 100,000 men; but under General von Seekt ways and means were found of circumventing these provisions. When Hitler came to power in early 1933 he had a firm foundation of illegal re-armament on which to build his armed forces.

In the old Imperial Army the influence of the Guards and the cavalry had far exceeded their actual numbers and this situation lingered on into the Third Reich, although it tended to become diluted by the emergence of younger officers dedicated to National Socialism. In 1939 roughly one-third of serving generals had the *von* in front of their names, indicating nobility – although in England most of them would have ranked as country gentry. In addition, the majority came from northern Germany, the traditional Prussian territories.

It would be fair to state that most senior officers welcomed the advent of Hitler, with the proviso that they imagined that they would be able to control him. Indeed, most of them despised the jumped-up corporal, but he was dedicated to rebuilding the German armed forces. However, like the genie released from the bottle, he ended up controlling them.

In order to cement his power base Hitler needed the Army, and initially he was prepared to co-operate, even to the extent of suppressing his rival organisation, the SA. Its leader, Ernst Röhm, together with a number of his familiars, was eliminated in a bloody purge on 30 June 1934.

From then on the Army found itself on a slippery slope from which there was no escape. The early series of bloodless victories in the Rhineland, Austria and Czechoslovakia gave Hitler an aura of infallibility. It was this that made it possible for him in February 1938 to get rid of the two most senior generals, Blomberg and von Fritsch, and to conduct a general purge of the Army.

As war with France began to seem more and more likely, certain senior officers began to plot in a disjointed and irresolute fashion. They were torn between their repugnance towards a regime that they believed would lead Germany to ruin,

and their oath of loyalty to Hitler as head of state. It was this very oath that was to hamstring all efforts to remove the dictator.

The campaign in Poland was another easy victory, followed by the conquest of most of Scandinavia, the Low Countries and France. Hitler could say to his generals, 'I told you so'. Promotions and decorations were showered on the successful commanders – 12 field marshals were created in one day, thus cheapening the rank. Hitler increasingly took over the personal direction of the war, interfering even down to battalion level at times. For those who agreed with him promotion was swift, but downfall could be even more rapid. Men like von Rundstedt were frequently sacked, only to bounce back again, while others simply faded into oblivion.

The final catastrophe for the Army was the botched assassination attempt of 20 July 1944. A considerable number of generals were executed as a result, and what trust Hitler still retained in the abilities of the Army was finally broken.

After the war, emerging from Allied prison camps, many of the generals put pen to paper in attempts to justify their actions and attitudes, and most of them have laid the blame fully on the shoulders of Hitler. This naturally ignores the fact that the senior ranks in the Army were eager to participate in his conquests, and thus had to join him in defeat.

The 'Christian Navy' was in many ways a separate organisation and tended to remain so, initially under the total command of Raeder. Hitler had little understanding of the principles of maritime strategy. He expected too much from his capital ships, which achieved little during the war. It is ironic that his chosen successor should have been an admiral, Dönitz, who had to preside over the disintegration of the Reich.

Parallel to the Army was the Waffen-SS, which should not be confused with the Allgemeine-SS, the Gestapo or the SD. Originally conceived as an élite political gendarmerie, the Waffen-SS was increasingly committed to combat; it proved extremely effective on the field of battle, but its reputation has ever since been marred by atrocities perpetrated by a minority. However, the chronic manpower shortage caused by the losses in Russia led to a dilution. By 1944 the SS divisions were being filled up with conscripts, redeployed personnel of the other services, and large numbers of foreigners and ethnic Germans.[1]

The Luftwaffe was in many ways a creation of the Nazi Party. Forbidden to keep aircraft by the Treaty of Versailles, the Army lost interest in aviation between the wars. Although most of the founders were ex-Army officers the administration and supply evolved along different lines, largely as a result of Göring's influence. A man like Kesselring, however, could combine a Luftwaffe career with a senior appointment on the ground. The tragedy was that the Luftwaffe could not fulfil the promises made on its behalf by its commanders.

The Commanders

Colonel-General Josef 'Sepp' Dietrich

The rise of Hitler brought with it the rise of a large number of extremely unsavoury characters. For many historians, 'Sepp' Dietrich was one of the most unpleasant of these, a swaggering braggart who had been dragged up from the gutter, the very worst type of SS bully. However, to the impartial observer there is a certain attraction about Dietrich. Fanatically brave, he had a certain openness of character and an earthy charm of manner. Although an extreme proletarian he was accepted and even respected by many of the senior Army officers.

'Sepp' Dietrich was born in Bavaria in 1893 and spent part of his youth as a butcher's apprentice. In 1911 he joined the Bavarian Army and during the First World War rose to become a senior NCO in a tank unit, with a reputation for ruthlessness. As such he naturally drifted into the ranks of the Freikorps, and excelled in street fighting against Communists. In the scattered array of nationalist groups in Munich he came to the attention of Hitler and was one of his earliest followers. More or less a founder member of the SS, which was formed to protect party

[1] See Men at Arms 34 (Revised) *The Waffen-SS.*

Joseph 'Sepp' Dietrich, on Himmler's left in this pre-war group, commanded the premier combat formation of the Waffen-SS throughout the war. This photo showing him in the black pre-war service dress of the SS is a useful reminder that the bluff, brave, hard-mouthed tank general described by von Rundstedt as 'decent, but stupid' owed his promotion to ruthless support of Hitler in the bloody period of political gang-warfare. There is deep irony in his earliest recorded civilian trade – butcher's apprentice. (Imp. War Mus.)

meetings, he functioned as the chief bouncer; and incredible as it may seem, by 1933 he was the equivalent in the SS of a major-general. In the same year he took command of Hitler's 'household bodyguard', the 'Leibstandarte Adolf Hitler', and with his troops played a leading part in the arrest and murder of Röhm and the other SA leaders in June 1934. Dietrich was in charge of the execution squad at the Stadelheim prison in Munich.

In the period before the war he continued to command the bodyguard as part of the still-small SS, which remained a purely Party formation. For prestige purposes, however, it was necessary for the Party's private army to go to war, and ex-sergeant-major Dietrich led the 'LAH' at motorised regimental strength in the campaign in the West in 1940. His unit came under the command of Guderian and fought well in the advance to the Channel. Dietrich was usually in the thick of the fight, and he was nearly killed when his car was shot up. It was at this stage in his career that the propaganda legend began to blossom. Dietrich was God's gift to Goebbels, who was always trying to boost the SS at the expense of the Army. He was turned into a sort of Germanic version of Superman, and Hitler thought highly of him.

The 'LAH' was uprated to divisional strength and received the best equipment available. Dietrich commanded it in Greece and then in Russia with great success, gaining the grudging respect of the Army. As a divisional commander, however, he had reached the limit of his talents, and by the end of 1943 most of his original comrades had been killed or captured.

In 1944 he was moved to the West to take command of 1st SS Panzer Corps, directly under von Rundstedt – who thought him stupid. When the invasion came on 6 June 1944 the German commanders were caught unprepared. Dietrich was in charge of the armoured counter-attacks in the Caen area, but the fortunes of war had changed. Allied air superiority made movement almost impossible, and it was at this stage that disillusionment began to set in. He was to become more and more openly critical of Hitler.

After the failure of the July bomb plot he was again promoted, to command the newly formed 5th Panzer Army on the Caen front, but his force was weakened by the removal of armoured units for the Avranches counter-attack. Barely extricating a small percentage of their strength from the Falaise pocket, his units started back to the Seine on the long retreat, minus most of their vehicles.

His next assignment was to command the 6th SS Panzer Army for the Ardennes offensive, in which he had no share of the planning and in which he did not believe. As a result of the bomb plot the main strength was given to the SS, although Dietrich was not the man to command an army. The initial success proved illusory and was marred by the activities of some members of Jochen Peiper's mobile column, which did little to enhance the reputation of the SS.

In spite of the failure of the attack Dietrich was sent in January 1945, with the remains of his 6th SS Panzer Army, to try to build up a front

Dönitz, seen here in the uniform of Grossadmiral, learned from his operational experience in the 1914–18 War that concentrations of U-boats were a more effective weapon against Allied convoys than unco-ordinated attacks by single submarines. He devised the 'Wolf Pack' tactics which came close to inflicting unacceptable shipping losses on Great Britain, and Churchill later wrote that this was the Axis weapon which came closest to causing him to despair. A popular and inspiring commander of no very great intellectual attainments, Dönitz was defeated by a combination of successful Allied radio-decode intelligence and improved anti-submarine detection equipment. His own son was lost on U-boat operations in the Atlantic. (Imp. War Mus.)

against the Russians in Hungary. He was driven back into Austria; and in the closing stages of the war Hitler ordered certain of the old SS divisions to be stripped of their prestigious unit armbands, including the 'LAH'. Dietrich was furious, and according to an apocryphal but characteristic legend, he packed his decorations in a chamber pot and sent them back to the Führer.

In 1946 he was sentenced to life imprisonment for war crimes by the Allies, but was released on parole in 1955. Two years later he was again on trial, this time before a West German court, charged with aiding manslaughter at the time of the Röhm purge – for which he received eighteen months. Aged 74, this colourful character died in 1966 at Ludwigsburg.

Grand Admiral Karl Dönitz

Dönitz is chiefly remembered as the founder and leader of the German submarine service and as the last 'Führer' of Nazi Germany. Arraigned as a war criminal in the dock at Nürnberg, he was aquitted of the charge of waging the submarine war in a criminal manner. Until his recent death he lived in retirement in North Germany and was often visited by his erstwhile enemies. At his recent funeral a large number of veterans turned out to pay their respects to their wartime leader.

Karl Dönitz was born in Berlin in September 1891 and attended grammar school. At the age of 18 he entered the Imperial Navy as a cadet and was promoted lieutenant in September 1913. When war broke out he was serving on the light cruiser *Breslau*, which together with the *Goeben* broke through the Allied blockade in the Mediterranean and reached Istanbul. Remaining in Turkey, he took part in operations in the Black Sea and even flew as an observer over the site of the Gallipoli landings. In autumn 1916 he returned to Germany emblazoned with both Iron Crosses, and applied to join the submarine service. After serving as a watch officer he was given his own boat – UC25 – in March 1918. Later in the year, while in command of UB-68, he attacked a convoy in the Mediterranean. His boat was damaged and he and his crew were taken prisoner by the British Navy.

Dönitz was released in July 1919 and joined the Reichsmarine as commander of a torpedo boat. By the late 1920s he was a commander and a qualified staff officer; and during this time he wrote a number of studies on submarine warfare, trying to persuade his superiors to consider rebuilding the submarine service – forbidden to Germany under the provisions of the Treaty of Versailles.

Hitler's rise to power gave him his chance, and while serving as captain of the cruiser *Emden* in 1934 he was given the job of building up a submarine force from scratch, based on Kiel. He achieved wonders in a short period, but his demands for a large force were not met. His superior, Raeder, together with the Nazi hierarchy, were more interested in the prestige value of large battleships. Thus at the beginning of the war in 1939 Germany had only 57 submarines, and only 26 of them were fit for long-range operations.

Their success, however, was out of all proportion to their numbers, and Dönitz proved an inspiring leader who was looked on almost as a father by the U-boat crews. He developed the concept of mass attack on convoys by the so-called 'wolf pack', and the development of a central control system fed by information from long-range aircraft.

The impressive amount of tonnage sunk, however, brought America more and more into the war, forcing her into a position of offensive neutrality. The United States took over convoy escort duties and lent destroyers to Britain, helping to keep the Atlantic lifeline open. American ingenuity was applied to shipbuilding, and the Allied nations developed sophisticated underwater detection systems.

By early 1943 the tide had turned and the strategic threat from the German U-boats had been defeated. Dönitz, who had been promoted and decorated lavishly in the early years of the war, was called to higher office. Raeder, the head of the German Navy, was relieved in March 1942 and Dönitz was appointed as his successor; retaining at the same time command of the submarines, he was promoted to grand admiral.

Dönitz spent much of the latter period of the war in close proximity to Hitler, who trusted him. However, his dreams of building up a new modern submarine fleet were doomed to failure on account of the lack of resources. New and more powerful boats were built, but their losses were far greater than the damage they achieved, although right to the end the crews continued loyal to the man they called their 'great lion'. With the High Seas Fleet either sunk or immobilised in Norway, Dönitz became more and more a figurehead, making propaganda speeches at factory meetings and urging National Socialist unity.

In the middle of April 1945 he was placed in command of all German forces in northern Europe, while still sending out his U-boats to almost certain doom. On 30 April he received a signal informing him that Hitler was dead and had nominated him as his successor with the title of Reichspresident. To his credit he immediately shrugged off the Nazi image and became again a capable officer, organising the rescue of thousands of refugees from the Baltic coast before they were overrun by the Russians. This was the last service performed by the remnant of his once-proud fleet.

'Fast Heinz' Guderian flanked by Panzer officers on the French coast after his dazzling advance to the sea in summer 1940. (Imp. War Mus.)

One of the main accused at Nürnberg, Dönitz was convicted of preparation for a war of aggression but received the comparatively mild sentence of ten years, all of which he served in Spandau prison. One of his fellow inmates, Albert Speer, referred to him as a lieutenant-commander who had been promoted too rapidly. Karl Dönitz died on Christmas Day 1980.

Colonel-General Heinz Guderian

In connection with the development of armoured warfare, the name of Guderian will never be forgotten. Indeed, his reputation seems to have become almost a legend although he never reached the highest rank in the German Army. He was a difficult man to control and the only one of his contemporaries who dared to stand up to Hitler and even to violently contradict him. A devoted apostle of 'blitzkrieg', he was renowned among the troops for his drive and dash in leading his Panzer formations from the front. Like Patton, he was always prepared to turn a blind eye to orders in which he did not believe.

Heinz Guderian was born at Chulm, on the Vistula, in 1888 and joined the Army in 1907 as a cadet. During the First World War he became a signals specialist, served in various staff appointments and briefly commanded an infantry battalion. After the war he remained in the Reichswehr, and turned his attention to the possibilities of mechanised warfare. It would be an exaggeration to state that he was the founder of Germany's Panzer divisions, but he was deeply involved from the beginning in their development. He was greatly influenced by the writings of Liddell-Hart and Fuller during the 1920s, translating several articles into German. His superiors in the Army, however, were not particularly impressed.

During the 1920s he worked closely with the then-Colonel Lutz of the Inspectorate of Motorised Troops, and spent three years as an instructor. Guderian's enthusiasms were frequently dampened by the lack of interest of his superiors. In 1931 he was promoted to lieutenant-colonel and became chief-of-staff to Lutz, who was by then a general. Guderian was responsible for the introduction of the first primitive tanks in Germany, but his real chance came in 1933 with the Nazi seizure of power. That year they were demonstrated to Hitler, who expressed great enthusiasm; and in 1935 the first three Panzer divisions were formed. Guderian was given command of 2nd Panzer and was promoted to major-general. In 1938 Lutz was sacked in the general purge and Guderian stepped into his shoes as a lieutenant-general. In this capacity he was in charge of the first campaign of the new formations, the 'invasion' of Austria, during which many of the untried vehicles broke down.

For the campaign in Poland Guderian was given command of XIX Corps, a largely mechanised formation, which he led from the front in dashing style all the way to Brest-Litovsk. He thus earned one of the earliest Knight's Crosses. General of Panzer Troops Guderian then had to transfer his corps to the West to prepare for the attack on France. During the 'Phoney War' the lessons learned in Poland were digested, and on 10 May 1940 Guderian was in command of three Panzer divisions. The story of the breakthrough at Sedan and the dash to the Channel is well known. Working in close co-operation with his 'flying artillery' – the Stukas – and occasionally ignoring orders to stop, he handled his corps in a way which was to establish him as one of the great armoured leaders. He finished the campaign by leading the advance to the Swiss border which cut France in half.

He was promoted to colonel-general in July but then found himself virtually unemployed until 1941, being engaged in training new armoured units. As he later wrote, his opinion on the future course of the war 'was not sought'.

Guderian was horrified when he heard about the plan to invade Russia, not on moral grounds but on account of purely military considerations. However, he accepted command of the 2nd Panzer Group, which comprised five armoured divisions and three motorised infantry divisions, divided into two corps. The initial successes were impressive, as he smashed through to the Dnieper in only 15 days and romped on towards Moscow. He was firmly of the opinion that Moscow should have been taken 'on the run', but other advice was to prevail. As it was, although his reconnaissance troops got into the outskirts of the capital in early December, the Russian counter-attack forced him to break off and go onto the defensive. He demanded of Hitler that his troops, unequipped for winter warfare, be allowed to retire to better positions, a demand which was naturally refused. Later in the month he quarrelled bitterly with his superior, von Kluge, and was relieved of his command.

He thus joined the increasing group of un-employed generals for over a year, and it was not until March 1943 that he was given the post of Inspector-General of Armoured Forces. In that capacity he was frequently in contact with Hitler and never failed to present his views forcefully, although usually without success. It is clear that his active mind was occupied with questions of future strategy at that time.

When the bomb attempt took place in July 1944 he was taken by surprise, never having had any contact with the plotters. In the immediate aftermath he was involved in the Court of Honour that expelled the plotters from the Army, and was then appointed Chief of the General Staff. In this position he exercised no real influence on the course of the war, and after a violent disagreement with Hitler was again dismissed in March 1945.

Never tried as a war criminal, Guderian retired to write his memoirs and died in 1954.

Kesselring as an Air Fleet commander in 1940. As Supreme Commander South his wide responsibilities sometimes caused friction between himself and Rommel, his often-impetuous subordinate. Rommel's constant demands for air support and convoy escorts drew some stinging replies, and his staff were secretly delighted when Kesselring came under RAF attack during one visit to the desert, their delight turning to rapture when Kesselring leapt into a slit trench that had been used for kitchen refuse . . . (Imp. War Mus.)

Field Marshal Albert Kesselring

Kesselring was in many ways an exception to the general rule of senior German officers. He was one of the few who was never sacked, even temporarily; he came to prominence in the Luftwaffe although he had served in the Army during the First World War, and he ended up as Supreme Commander West. He did not come from a military family (his father was a schoolmaster); he was a Bavarian and originally an artilleryman.

Albert Kesselring was born in November 1885 in northern Bavaria, and after attending grammar school at Bayreuth entered a Bavarian artillery regiment in 1904 as an officer cadet. His service during the First World War was undistinguished, a mixture of staff and troop command appointments, and he ended with the rank of captain. The same applied to his activities in the Reichswehr during the 1920s and early '30s when he filled a series of administrative posts.

Kesselring entered the still-secret Luftwaffe right at the start in late 1933, having left the Army as a colonel. From then on his rise was spectacular. Although a friend of Göring's, he deserved his promotions. In 1935 he took over the entire non-technical administration of the Luftwaffe, and the following year he was appointed chief-of-staff. During this period he was

9

mainly responsible for cancelling the heavy bomber programme in which he did not believe.

When war broke out Kesselring was in command of Air Fleet I in Poland, where his mission was to support the ground troops of von Bock's army group. Within the concept of 'blitzkrieg' as the Germans understood it this co-operation was vital, in that aircraft fulfilled the rôle of flying artillery. From Poland Kesselring moved to the West to take over Air Fleet 2; his aircraft, again in support of von Bock, played a vital rôle in the victory in France and the Low Countries. He was, however, unable to make good Göring's boast that air power could decimate the British retreat from Dunkirk.

For the remainder of 1940 Kesselring was in charge of the air force that attempted to win air superiority over Britain. He was promoted to field marshal in the general hand-out of batons in July, and unlike many of his colleagues he was enthusiastic about the chances for Operation 'Sea Lion' – the invasion of England. 'Sea Lion' and the Battle of Britain faded into insignificance in the shadow of Hitler's plans to conquer Russia, however, and in the spring of 1941 Kesselring and his 2nd Air Fleet were transferred to the East. There he again worked together with von Bock's ground forces.

Most people connect Italy with the name of Kesselring. In December 1941 he was appointed Supreme Commander South and moved his headquarters to Rome. In this capacity he commanded all the German forces in southern Europe – including Rommel's Afrikakorps. However, this was still primarily an air appointment and Kesselring's main task was to organise the supply of the troops in Africa, to deal with Malta and to keep the sea routes open in the Mediterranean.

Active command of ground troops came in July 1943, when Italy surrendered and the Allies invaded the mainland. Initially he had two armies, and from then until early 1945 he conducted the brilliant series of defensive battles up the leg of Italy that so effectively slowed the Allied advance. During this period his priority in terms of supplies and manpower was low and he had to make do with what he had got. For his handling of the early stages of the battle he was

Günther von Kluge (left) earned Hitler's favour by a hard-driving style of leadership, but his attitude to the anti-Hitler resistance group among the generals was ambiguous. A difficult colleague, 'clever Hans' once challenged Guderian to a duel with pistols – with Hitler as his second! (Imp. War Mus.)

awarded the Diamonds for his already impressively garnished Knight's Cross.

The final promotion came in March 1945 after von Rundstedt had been sacked for the last time. Kesselring was appointed Supreme Commander West – far too late to stand any chance of stabilising the crumbling front along the Rhine.

Although highly regarded by Allied commanders as a decent opponent, in early 1947 he was tried by the British as a war criminal and sentenced to death for the shooting of partisans by troops under his command. This sentence caused some high-level protests; he was reprieved, and was released from prison in 1952 on account of ill health. He died in retirement at Bad Wiessee in July 1960. In an obituary his erstwhile opponent, the American General Mark Clark, referred to him as one of the most capable of Hitler's officers. In 1954 his autobiography *A Soldier's Record* was published, which gives a fair and balanced view of his career.

Field Marshal Günther von Kluge

Nicknamed by fellow officers 'clever Hans', von Kluge was a specially gifted tactician whose early career had been spectacular. Under Hitler he rose again rapidly, and it is his relations with the latter that still leave a question mark hanging over his character. On one occasion he stated that 'one should kill the swine', but that did not stop him from accepting a large money present from Hitler. Although he sympathised with the motives of the Resistance he resisted pressure to join them; and when he finally committed suicide after the failure of the bomb attempt he wrote an obsequious farewell letter to Hitler.

Günther von Kluge, often called Hans, was born into an Army family in October 1882; in 1913 the family were ennobled by the Kaiser. His father became a lieutenant-general, and both Günther and his brother joined the Prussian Cadet Corps. He passed out in 1901 and joined the artillery, where in his regiment there was a young lieutenant named Keitel.

From 1909 to 1912 he attended the war academy with such success that he was soon seconded to the General Staff. When the First World War began his position on the staff was made permanent and he was promoted captain. During the war he served on the Russian, Isonzo, Carpathian and Flanders fronts, winning both Iron Crosses, but was seriously wounded near Verdun in October 1918.

Von Kluge moved into the Reichswehr in 1919 and by 1923 was a major in the training department of the War Ministry. In 1927 he was promoted lieutenant-colonel, and two years later he was a full colonel commanding an artillery regiment. With the rise to power of Hitler he too rose swiftly. In 1933 he was made a major-general and Inspector of Signals, and the following year he was a lieutenant-general commanding the 6th Division. This unit was soon turned into the VI Korps, and its commander became a general of artillery in August 1936.

When war broke out in the summer of 1939 von Kluge was in command of 4th Army under von Bock for the invasion of Poland. This quick victory brought him the Knight's Cross and promotion to colonel-general, after which he transferred his army to the West. On 10 May 4th Army took part in the 'blitzkrieg' campaign as part of von Rundstedt's Army Group A. Von Kluge's army, with Rommel's 7th Panzer Division as spearhead, forced its way across the Meuse and through to the Channel coast. Rather than trying to stop his impetuous tank commanders, von Kluge tended to give them their head. This dash and determination was rewarded

with the marshal's baton in the general promotion of July 1940.

A year later von Kluge took his army into Russia and led it via Bialystok and Smolensk to the threshold of Moscow. There, in December, the advance bogged down and the Russians went over to the attack. In a general purge his army group commander, von Bock, was sacked and replaced by the two-years-younger and more dynamic von Kluge.

At this stage in his career he first came into contact with the active resistance in the person of General von Treskow, the nephew of his predecessor. He was in general agreement with the ideas of the plotters but declined to undertake anything against the head of state to whom he had sworn loyalty. However, he was prepared to defy Hitler's 'no withdrawal' orders on occasions. Through 1943 the plotters' efforts continued, to the extent that von Kluge agreed to act; but towards the end of November he was injured in a car accident and disappeared from the scene for six months. Who knows what might have happened in July 1944 if he had been behind the bomb plot instead of on the sidelines?

Von Kluge's next appointment was to attempt to stop the Allied invasion from expanding its bridgehead. At the beginning of July 1944 Hitler resolved to 'retire' von Rundstedt and replace him with the more adventurous von Kluge. Full of eagerness he set off for France; but once on the spot and in conference with Rommel, the new Supreme Commander West realised that the situation was hopeless. When the bomb attempt failed a few weeks later he did nothing, but was already out of favour with Hitler for not having produced the expected miracle. In addition (and quite without cause) the Führer thought that he might go over to the Allies.

This suspicion was resolved in mid-August when Berlin lost contact with him for a whole day. Hitler imagined that he had been secretly meeting with Allied officers to discuss surrender, and on the 17th Model arrived at his headquarters with a letter relieving him of his command. More ominously, he was ordered to report to Berlin. Realising that he had no chance, he took poison on the way back to Germany and died on 19 August 1944. In his farewell letter he urged Hitler to make peace while there was still a chance, but couched it in the most subservient of tones. It was this contrast between subservience and secret plotting that was the downfall and tragedy of the German officer corps.

Colonel-General Bruno Lörzer

Lörzer was in many ways typical of the group of World War I veterans who rose in the new Luftwaffe together with Göring. He owed his position and promotion to the patronage of the latter, and several historians have maintained that he was promoted way above the level of his ability. There is some justification in this, but he handled his formations well during the Battle of France in 1940. There have also been allegations of corruption, high living and looting from occupied countries. In this, however, he would only have been following the example set by his more illustrious master.

Bruno Lörzer was born in 1891 and joined the Imperial Army in 1910 as an infantry officer. Even in those early days he was passionately interested in flying, and when war broke out he managed to get himself seconded for pilot training. He had met Göring in 1912, but the latter stayed initially on the ground. Lörzer went to Freiburg to learn to fly, and in the early months of the war he was joined there by Göring, who had been wounded at the front. Without permission Göring joined the flying school and appointed himself Lörzer's observer. The two flew as a team for some months until Göring learnt to fly at his own expense and joined the squadron as a pilot. It is said that they each saved the other's life in air combat.

At the end of the war Lörzer was credited with 44 'kills', and was thus equal seventh in the list of German aces. Like many of his comrades he drifted into civil aviation, but kept in touch with Göring and later joined the Nazi Party. An Air Force was forbidden to Germany at the time, but many were busily circumventing this restriction. In 1935 Lörzer was head of the National Socialist Flying Corps (NSFK) and transferred into the fledgling Luftwaffe, which was desperately in need of experienced personnel. By 1939 he was a lieutenant-general commanding II Air Corps. (The NSFK was a uniformed offshoot of the Nazi Party and its aim was to provide flying training in civilian aircraft for air-minded young people. It served as a nucleus upon which the Luftwaffe could be rapidly expanded when it was formed in 1935.)

In the spring of 1940 Lörzer's air corps took part in the invasion of France, where its main mission was to fly sorties in support of Gunderian's Panzer Group. Lörzer was keen enough to stage army-air co-operation exercises and he frequently discussed combined operations with Guderian in person. They agreed that for the crossing of the Meuse at Sedan on 13 May the air corps would fly continuous support missions; but Kleist, the army commander, changed this at the last minute to a mass bombing attack to coincide with the artillery bombardment. However, when his attack started Guderian noticed that the aircraft were carrying out the tactics that he had agreed with Lörzer. When he questioned him later Lörzer said that von Kleist's orders had arrived 'too late'. To implement them would have 'confused the squadrons'.

After the fall of France II Air Corps was based mainly in the Pas de Calais, where it flew missions over the Channel and bombed targets in southern England. If Operation 'Sea Lion' had been mounted Lörzer's aircraft would have been responsible for covering the crossing of the Channel and for providing close support after the landings.

Following their failure to win air superiority during the autumn of 1940, the Germans cancelled 'Sea Lion' and the great movement to the East began. In summer 1941 II Air Corps took part in the invasion of Russia as part of Kesselring's 2nd Air Fleet. Their mission was to support the ground forces of von Bock's Army Group Centre. In October, however, Lörzer's forces were moved to Italy. He established his headquarters at Messina in Sicily, from where he was responsible for keeping open the sea communications with the forces in North Africa. Like many other Luftwaffe commanders he was over-optimistic about the effects of air bombardment. In the spring of 1942 he boasted that Malta had been completely eliminated as a base for air and sea operations.

In 1943 he was forced to move back to the

mainland by the Allied invasion, and spent the rest of the war in the Italian theatre. It was from his lengthy period of service there that the allegations of corruption stemmed, and also the accusations of incompetence.

A final paradox is that he refused to give evidence on behalf of his friend, Göring, when the latter was in the dock at Nürnberg.

Field Marshal Erich von Manstein

Military historians are more or less unanimous in their opinion that von Manstein was the most competent of the German commanders during the Second World War. Marshal Malinovski once wrote: 'We regarded the hated Erich von Manstein as our most dangerous opponent. His technical mastery of every situation was incomparable.'

He was born Erich von Lewinski in Berlin in November 1887, but he was brought up by and later adopted by an aunt who was married to a certain Major von Manstein – the name he subsequently took. (Both the Lewinskis and Mansteins were old military families, but some suspicion of Jewish ancestry clung to the former, which did not go down too well in certain Nazi circles.)

With such a background it was natural that the young Erich should make his way through the Prussian cadet academies, and he entered the Army in 1906. As a nobleman he joined a Foot Guard regiment in Berlin, and was a senior lieutenant by the time the First World War started, having passed out from the war academy.

He fought in the early battles with a reserve regiment of the Guards and in November 1914 he was severely wounded. Promoted captain in 1915, he served for the rest of the period of hostilities as a staff officer. During the 1930s he continued mainly in staff appointments interspersed with short periods in command of troops. In 1932, as a lieutenant-colonel, he was in Russia to observe the manoeuvres of the Red Army.

In 1936 he was promoted to major-general and worked on the staff to further the development of tanks and assault guns; but when the Army was purged in February 1938 he was sent off to command an infantry division in the provinces with the rank of lieutenant-general.

Erich von Manstein in 1940, as a brilliant planner and commander of XXXVIII Infantry Corps; he proposed the hook through the Ardennes which was to be the ruin of the Allied defences, and under his command the infantry proved to be a tough and flexible weapon, almost keeping up with the tanks. This photo provides an interesting contrast to those taken three years later, when his face was deeply etched by the fatigue and responsibility of command in Russia.

When war broke out he was chief-of-staff to von Rundstedt's army group and as such he took part in the Polish invasion, after which they were moved to the West. It was at this time that he first came to prominence as the originator of the plan to break through the French defences in the Ardennes. This idea found no favour at all with the army high command, who decided to get rid of this awkward staff officer by promoting him to command a corps in the East. However, on his way to take up his new appointment he dined with Hitler and spoke about his ideas – which Hitler promptly adopted.

Von Manstein took part with his corps in the campaign in France, and won the Knight's Cross and promotion to general of infantry in June 1940. The following year he was in command of a Panzer corps at the outset of the campaign in Russia, and in five days at the end of June he penetrated 150 miles to Dvinsk.

Von Manstein rose rapidly under the conditions of the Eastern Front. Just over two months after the campaign started he was appointed to command 11th Army, and was told to capture the Crimea. In spite of reverses during the first Russian winter he managed to capture the fortress of Sevastopol, for which he was given his field marshal's baton in July 1942. However, an attempt to stage a repeat performance against Leningrad failed and was abandoned. In November von Manstein was appointed to command Army Group Don.

As an army group commander in Russia he was responsible for defending a front of some 600 miles with an average of 60 divisions, thus controlling far more men than any Allied army group commander during the war. This promotion, however, was the beginning of his downfall, because Hitler was in charge by then and von Manstein was not the type to simply take orders.

His immediate problem was Stalingrad, where he was unable to relieve the encircled 6th Army; and from then on the retreat began. Von Manstein repeatedly urged Hitler to shorten the front to conserve manpower, but he was up against the Führer's obstinate refusal to abandon territory. By March 1944 his headquarters was back on the Polish border and at the end of the month he was sacked, never to be re-employed during the war.

Hitler's criticism was that he was an operational general, unable to conduct a retreat and a defensive, which was an unjust over-simplification. He was never given the chance to prove his capabilities on account of the constant interference from above.

The final injustice was that von Manstein was charged with war crimes before a British court in 1949 and was sentenced to 18 years' imprisonment. The basis for the charges was complicity in murders carried out behind the lines in Russia by SS extermination squads. It is pleasant to record that his defence was paid for by a group of British officers who justly disagreed with the decision to try von Manstein.

After a serious eye operation he was released from prison in 1953, and was the only one of Hitler's field marshals who was asked to help in the foundation of the modern German army. In retirement he wrote two books of memoirs.

Hermann Hoth, a General of Infantry in 1939, proved himself a Panzer expert in France and Russia; in Operation 'Barbarossa' his 3rd Panzer Group encircled hundreds of thousands of Russians in the Vyazma-Bryansk pocket. 'Papa' Hoth, a cool and popular commander, had perhaps his finest hour in the third battle of Kharkov after the fall of Stalingrad, when he and Manstein crushed a Soviet attack and inflicted losses of 32,000 men and 600 tanks. At Kursk in July 1943 Hoth commanded the largest force of German armour ever assembled; the failure of the attack was inevitable, but Hoth might have been able to salvage a sort of victory out of the tank battle of Prokorovkha had Hitler not intervened. Kursk was used as the excuse to sack him from command of his 4th Panzer Army in December 1943.

He died aged 85 in July 1973, and was buried with full military honours at Dorrmark.

General of Panzer Troops Hasso von Manteuffel

In any generation of German military history the name of Manteuffel is to be found well to the fore. Hasso von Manteuffel was the last of a long line of distinguished forebears, and as one of the younger commanders produced by Germany during the Second World War, has since been regarded as one of the more able. He learnt his trade in the vastness of Russia, but suffered, like most of his contemporaries, from the stultifying influence of Hitler. He was as much of a Nazi as any of the German high command, and was untainted in the eyes of the Führer after the failure of the bomb plot. This did not prevent him, however, from making a valuable contribution in public life to the rebirth of the new Germany after the war.

Hasso von Manteuffel was born in 1897 and gravitated via the cadet academies into the Army, where he joined the cavalry. He took part in the tail end of the First World War and then moved into the Reichswehr. Between the wars he made no spectacular strides, but was one of the small group who were actively involved in the development of armoured forces during the later 1930s.

In the spring of 1941 he was given command of 7th Panzer Division, Rommel's old unit, and led it into Russia. This formed part of von Bock's Army Group Centre, and von Manteuffel took part in the advance to Moscow and the bitter winter battles in December of that year. Later he took over the élite 'Grossdeutschland' Panzer Division, also in Russia. He became an expert in manoeuvring large tank units, and in the earlier stages of the campaign his crews were of a high standard. Later, he was to suffer from Hitler's insistence on holding onto territory at all costs.

Still only a divisional commander, in early September 1944 Manteuffel was moved to the West. There he was to take command of the reconstituted 5th Panzer Army, which had been moved from Belgium to Strasbourg. Hitler was worried about the advance into Lorraine by General Patton's 3rd US Army and was determined to stage a powerful counter-attack. Manteuffel's mission was to stop Patton in front of the Vosges.

This swift promotion from a division to an army was not all it seemed, however. The German armed forces in the autumn of 1944 were but a shadow of their former power, and most of the tanks had been destroyed in the retreat from the Normandy battles. Manteuffel took over a somewhat motley force. Although lacking in artillery and in vehicles, he was ordered to attack on 18 September to capture Lunéville and then to throw the Americans back across the Moselle. He carried out his orders with

misgivings, and in a four-day tank battle suffered considerable losses – mainly from American aircraft strikes. Manteuffel was strongly criticised by his army group commander, Blaskowitz, for not having shown enough determination, but in the event it was Blaskowitz who was sacked as a result.

5th Panzer Army was disengaged from the Lorraine front in early October and sent to the rear to refit for the coming Ardennes offensive. Manteuffel's army was to be in the centre of the advance, which aimed to cross the Meuse and advance towards Antwerp. He himself, in common with both his superiors, von Rundstedt and Model, was not particularly enthusiastic about the plan, and would have preferred a less ambitious goal.

It was his army that actually enjoyed the greatest success in the early stages of the operation, and in spite of failing to capture Bastogne it might well have done better. Advance units actually reached the Meuse near Dinant, but the battles around Bastogne steadily absorbed more and more of the reinforcements that were belatedly sent in. Manteuffel was in the end severely defeated in the Ardennes, but cannot be entirely blamed. His forces were ill-equipped and many of the new units were only semi-trained. It was Hitler's insistence that Dietrich's SS units on the right wing should bear the brunt of attack that was at fault, as the chances of exploitation in the centre were far better.

As it was, when the skies cleared and the counter-attack started, the 5th Panzer Army was severely mauled. Later it was transferred to the East, where the Russians had broken through in Poland. After this even the capable Manteuffel no longer had any chance of influencing events.

After the war he emerged unscathed from the de-Nazification process, and in 1953 he was elected a member of the federal parliament for Neuss, a town on the Rhine near Düsseldorf. He served in this capacity until he retired in 1957. General von Manteuffel died in 1978.

Field Marshal Walter Model

Model liked to refer to himself as Hitler's 'fireman', always being posted to where things were burning. When promoted in early 1944 he was

Model was a commander of enormous energy and drive; junior leaders were sometimes startled to find him taking local control and leading their counter-attacks in person. He was not an easy man to work with, and his suicide reflected the fact that he had nailed his colours to the mast of the Third Reich; but he demonstrated repeatedly an almost unparalleled ability to stabilise the shuddering Eastern Front. On one occasion he arrived in a crisis to be asked by two senior officers what forces he had brought to plug the ruptured front. His reply was an icy glance through his monocle and the bark, 'Myself!' (Imp. War Mus.)

the youngest field marshal in the German Army, and certainly one of the most able. He was a master of the defensive battle and an inspired leader of troops, who rose from command of a division in the summer of 1941 to the leadership (at times) of virtually half of the Eastern Front. Model was one of the younger professional officers who owed their rise to the favour of Hitler, but he was quite prepared to argue with the Führer. Never really popular except with his men, who regarded him as lucky, he was a difficult subordinate and superior.

Walter Model was born in January 1891 in humble circumstances, but was a clever scholar at grammar school. Not particularly strong as a

youth, he had a difficult time during training as a cadet, but in 1910 he passed out as an infantry lieutenant. In the trenches during the First World War he was a keen soldier and was twice wounded, and in 1916 he was seconded for training for the General Staff. The following year he was promoted captain and spent the rest of the war as a staff officer with various units.

In 1918 Model stayed on in the Reichswehr and during the 1920s worked in a number of mainly administrative positions. As a major in 1931 he spent several weeks in Russia; and in 1934 he was a colonel commanding a regiment. The following year he returned to Berlin to take charge of a technical department concerned with new inventions, and played a major part in the development of the infantry assault gun that was later used to such great effect by the German Army.

In 1938 Model was promoted to major-general and became chief-of-staff to a corps. In this capacity he served in Poland, and in the campaign in the West he was chief-of-staff to Busch's 16th Army. Towards the end of 1940, by then a lieutenant-general, Model took over as commanding officer of the 3rd Panzer Division.

In the summer of 1941 he stormed into Russia with this division, and promotions followed rapidly. In October he rose to general of armoured troops and took command of XXXI Panzer Korps in front of Moscow; two months later he was in command of the 9th Army. Model sorted out the crisis of that winter, and the higher classes of the Knight's Cross were showered upon him, as well as promotion to colonel-general (February 1942). Hitler referred to him as the 'saviour of the Eastern Front', and Model certainly led his army with flair and determination, frequently in the front line and under fire.

However, the honeymoon did not last long. After Stalingrad Model protested that the troops were not capable of a further offensive, and in November 1943 he was sacked and sent home. This could easily have meant the end of a brilliant career, but two months later he was back in Russia. When Army Group North got into difficulties von Küchler was sacked, and Model was sent to clear up the situation – a task in which he succeeded and which brought him promotion to field marshal. At the end of March he was again transferred when von Manstein was sacked, and took over two army groups, North Ukraine and South. In June he replaced Busch in command of Army Group Centre but still retained control over Army Group North Ukraine. Model thus commanded more than a hundred divisions at one time – which should be compared with Eisenhower's fifty-odd divisions in 1945. Time and time again he succeeded in closing gaping holes in the Eastern Front, but the end was in sight as his troops were forced back into Poland and Czechoslovakia.

In August 1944 Model again was sent to a critical front, this time in the West, where he was to take over as Supreme Commander and commander of Army Group B from von Kluge – who promptly committed suicide. Model struggled against the Allies' advance with insufficient resources as he frantically tried to stabilise the front, sending off a stream of vain demands for reinforcements. In early September von Rundstedt was 're-activated' as Supreme Commander, but Model retained Army Group B. In the same month, as the man on the spot, he organised the defeat of the attempt to seize the bridge at Arnhem.

Model was never a believer in the Ardennes offensive, but was forced to carry it out, which led to a further weakening of his ill-equipped forces. He wanted to retire to prepare a defensive along the Rhine, but was naturally overruled by Hitler, who refused to give up an inch of territory. Through the early months of 1945 Model's armies were forced back across the Rhine and were finally surrounded in the Rühr Pocket in April. The Germans fought on in a hopeless situation, but surrender was unavoidable. Fearing that he would be handed over to the Russians as a war criminal, Model committed suicide on 21 April 1945 in a small wood near Düsseldorf.

Field Marshal Erwin Rommel

Wavell once compared Rommel to Wellington, and even during the war he was almost as popular with the 8th Army as was Montgomery. The British regarded him as a gentleman, and, unlike the rest of the German generals, he has been the subject of a considerable number of

Rommel receives a briefing on the Atlantic Wall defences early in 1944. It was largely due to his energy in stripping old 1940-vintage French and Belgian defences that the vaunted image spread by the propaganda service was transformed into a genuinely formidable defence line by June 1944, when it almost withstood the US landings at Omaha Beach. (Personality Picture Library)

biographies. In West Germany today he is fêted as a hero of the resistance to Hitler, and they have even named a warship after him. The paradox is, however, that he remained a convinced Nazi supporter and that his rise was almost entirely due to Hitler's favour. His dubious connection with the resistance rests entirely on the fact that his name was found by the Gestapo on a list made out by one of the plotters of possible collaborators: in view of his popularity with the Allies he was to have been given a high command in the Army after Hitler had been eliminated. This cooler view of the facts does not detract, however, from his undoubted capability as a leader of armoured formations, nor from his soldierly behaviour in war.

Erwin Rommel was born in Württemberg in November 1891 into a middle-class family, and after attending grammar school he entered the Army as a cadet in 1910. Two years later he passed out as a lieutenant into a Württemberg infantry regiment, and went to war in 1914 as a platoon commander. He spent the war entirely as a junior troop commander, taking part in the early battles on the Western Front, where he was wounded. In the autumn of 1915 he was transferred to a newly-formed mountain battalion and took part in the fighting on several fronts, including the Dolomites. During the Battle of the Isonzo he was responsible for the capture of Monte Matajur, for which he was awarded the Pour la Mérite. In 1918 he was promoted a captain – which he was to remain for the following fifteen years.

He spent the 1920s as a company commander, and without General Staff qualifications he was looked down upon by his superiors. (As late as 1943 von Rundstedt regarded him as 'little more than a divisional commander'.) In 1929, however, he was sent to Dresden to the War School as an instructor in tactics, a task for which he was particularly suited on the basis of his practical experience. During the 1930s his promotion was steady – major in 1933, lieutenant-colonel in 1935, colonel in 1937 and major-general in 1939. In 1937 he published a book on infantry tactics which found a wide readership and impressed Hitler.

For most of 1939 Rommel was in command of Hitler's headquarters troops, and as a reward he asked for and got, command of 7th Panzer Division. He led his division to war on 10 May 1940, and stamped his own highly original and personal system of command firmly in the minds of his officers. Leading from in front and frequently out of touch with his staff, narrowly avoiding capture on a number of occasions, Rommel stormed across the Meuse and on into Normandy.

Like Patton, he was in his element in a fluid warfare situation; and this ability he took with him to the Western Desert in early 1941. He was sent there by Hitler with only two divisions to stop the Italian collapse, and within weeks of his arrival the whole situation had changed. He was promoted to lieutenant-general, and his Afrika Korps chased the British from Cyrenaica back over the Egyptian border. As a result he was loaded with honours – in January 1942 he became a colonel-general and his command was enlarged as the Panzergruppe Afrika. The capture of Tobruk in June brought a marshal's baton for the 'Desert Fox', but the end was in sight in the material sense. Defeated at Alam-el-Halfa and El Alamein, he was down to a handful of tanks

as the long retreat to Tunisia began, sandwiched between Montgomery and the forces which had landed in Algeria. Before the final capitulation, however, Rommel was evacuated from Africa on health grounds and sent on leave in March 1943.

Later in the year he took over command of Army Group B in northern Italy, a situation in which he was unable to use his particular talent for mobile warfare; and in November 1943 he was sent to the West to study the defences of the Atlantic Wall. There he became embroiled in a conflict with his superior, von Rundstedt, about where the defensive emphasis should be placed. Rommel wanted the available armour well to the front, to defeat the Allied landings on the beaches, but von Rundstedt and OKW wanted them kept well back as a mobile reserve.

In December 1944 Rommel's position was regularised in that he was made responsible as an army group commander under Rundstedt for the defence of the coastline from the Scheldt to the Spanish frontier. Fully recovered from his illness, he threw his restless energy into building beach defences. However, Rommel was in charge only in name and was subject to constant interference from Berlin. When the invasion came he was absent from the front on his way to Berchtesgaden. He rushed back to Normandy immediately, but was unable to decisively alter the tide of the battle. On 17 July his car was shot up by an Allied fighter and he was badly wounded; this ended his active career.

Towards the end he had certainly been approached by the plotters but was firmly against the assassination attempt, although it is possible that if it had succeeded he could well have emerged as a credible negotiator in the eyes of the Allies. As it was, his name was connected with the plot; and on 14 October 1944 emissaries from Hitler presented him with the alternatives – voluntary suicide, and safety and honour for his family, or arrest and 'trial' for them all. A few hours later he took poison. The grisly deal was kept, and Rommel was given a state funeral.

Field Marshal Gerd von Rundstedt
Apart perhaps from Rommel, von Rundstedt was the best known of the senior German commanders during the Second World War. Photo-

Gerd von Rundstedt photographed as a Reichswehr general in the early 1930s, wearing the stand-and-fall grey collar of the period. Plate A2 illustrates his habitual uniform during the war years, with the collar and shoulder insignia of his status as 'Chef' or Colonel-in-Chief of the 18th Infantry. Only six general officers received these regimental honours, and they were highly prized. There are many stories testifying to von Rundstedt's dry sense of humour, and his ability to mimic practically every known German regional accent was used to cruel effect when he allowed himself to express an opinion of the Nazi upstarts he so despised. (Imp. War Mus.)

there were six von Rundstedts in the Imperial Army in 1913.

Gerd von Rundstedt was born in December 1875 at Aschersleben in Saxony, the son of a hussar officer who later became a major-general; and at the tender age of twelve he entered a cadet academy. At 17 he was commissioned as an ensign into an infantry regiment, in March 1892 – a year before Göring was born. From then on he followed the routine of peacetime soldiering, with regular promotions and entry into the General Staff as a captain in 1909. As a competent staff officer he served throughout the First World War, ending up as a major. Having survived the slaughter and with a wealth of experience he was chosen as one of those who would remain in the truncated Reichswehr. He was promoted lieutenant-colonel in command of an infantry regiment, and in 1923, as a full colonel, he returned to staff duties. Five and a half years before Hitler came to power he was a major-general.

He first appeared in the public eye in July 1932 when martial law was proclaimed in Berlin. This archetype of the non-political soldier was involved as military commander of the Berlin district in the expulsion of the social-democrat government and the occupation of the ministries.

In 1932 he was already a full general of infantry, and was far from being a supporter of the Nazis when they came to power. He often slightingly referred to Hitler as 'that Bohemian corporal', but this did not dissuade him from following his career. His first open disagreement with his new master came over the dismissal of von Fritsch in early 1938, and at his own request he was allowed to retire in October of that year.

With war brewing Hitler had need of every experienced officer, and he had a liking for the stiff Prussian nobleman. He was recalled in August 1939 to command Army Group North for the invasion of Poland. His contribution to the victory was rewarded with the Knight's Cross and the job of Supreme Commander East. However, he did not hold this post for long, as he strongly disagreed with the activities of the Party and the SS in occupied Poland. He asked to be re-assigned, and was sent to the West to command Army Group A.

graphs of him show a stern face with a high intelligent forehead. He always dressed in full uniform – he was never a 'character' in the sense of preferring outlandish dress – but usually wore the insignia of a regimental colonel rather than the oakleaves of a general on his collar. Outwardly typical of his caste, he had a sardonic sense of humour and spoke quite openly to Allied interrogators after the war. His family was Prussian with a long tradition of service to the state –

In the original planning for the attack in the West this group was subsidiary to that of von Bock in the north; but as a result of von Manstein's advocacy of the break-through in the Ardennes, it was gradually strengthened. When the attack started in May 1940, von Rundstedt commanded the Panzer groups which smashed their way to the Channel coast. Subsequently criticised for the fatal delay outside Dunkirk, von Rundstedt was given overall command of Operation 'Sea Lion', after the defeat of France. This was an operation in which he had little faith, and when it was finally abandoned he left to command Army Group South for the invasion of Russia in the summer of 1941.

The early victories were impressive and his 42 divisions overran vast areas of territory. However, as winter set in the Germans found themselves involved in a series of defensive battles. In December 1941 von Rundstedt asked permission to' withdraw for sound tactical reasons, but instead was dismissed.

This second period of retirement did not last long, and in March 1942 von Rundstedt was appointed Supreme Commander West. Already elderly, he took little part in affairs in occupied France where civilian labour gangs were building the Atlantic Wall. In the months preceding the invasion he differed over tactical method with Rommel, his immediate subordinate, but neither of them could free themselves from Hitler's supervision. When the invasion took place in June 1944 he made his most significant comment. Keitel telephoned him to ask what could be done, and von Rundstedt replied: 'Make peace, you idiots!' Probably as a result of this, he was again sacked on 6 July 1944.

Although in no way a Nazi he was never connected with the bomb plot. He even acted as president of the Court of Honour which expelled the plotters from the Army. In early September, however, he was again brought out of retirement and re-appointed as Supreme Commander West – with orders to stop the rot. He remained as a rather splendid figurehead, and it is an injustice to couple his name with the Ardennes offensive. He had nothing to do with the planning or execution of an operation in which he had no faith.

This portrait of Kurt Student shows to good effect the impressive gold-on-white collar patches of a Luftwaffe colonel-general. Eugen Meindl (see Plate G2) once said that Student 'had big ideas but not the faintest concept as to how they were to be carried out' – a disloyal remark for an officer who had been well treated by his superior, and one hard to reconcile with the evidence of Student's originality and energy as creator of the crack airborne forces. Men who did not know him sometimes mistook a characteristic slowness of speech for slowness of wit – an error which would have surprised his respectful and admiring enemies. (Imp. War Mus.)

His final dismissal came in March 1945, and two months later he was taken prisoner by the Americans. One of the few German commanders who was never tried for war crimes, he died at Celle in Hanover in February 1953.

Colonel-General Kurt Student

Student possessed one of the most original minds among the German leadership during the Second World War. He developed the concept of airborne troops long before the Allies had ever dreamt about them, and he proved to be an inspired leader. He was often accused of rashness and of having an excess of imagination by more conventionally-minded officers, but the opposite was the case. He was slow of speech and essentially thoughtful, and his planning for an operation was of the highest order.

Kurt Student was born in 1890. He saw front line service during the First World War which he ended as a captain, and he subsequently stayed on in the Reichswehr. In 1924 he was chosen to head the Air Technical Branch, and became involved with running gliding courses. This was one of the many subterfuges employed to circumvent the prohibition of an air force imposed upon Germany by the Treaty of Versailles.

His rise was hardly spectacular. By 1934 he was a colonel, but it was not until 1938 that he got his chance. Promoted to major-general, he was able to form a highly secret battalion of paratroops, which was expanded into a division the following year. This 7th Air Division was scheduled to make its first drop behind the Czech fortifications during the occupation of the rest of the country in the spring of 1939; this proved unnecessary – although it was later carried out successfully as an exercise.

The division did not take part in the Polish campaign in order to preserve secrecy, but was engaged in intensive training for the campaign in the Low Countries. Their main mission was to land inside 'Fortress Holland' to secure the airfields, but in the meantime they were suddenly switched to planning for operations in Scandinavia. On 9 April 1940, airborne forces secured the key airfields at Oslo and Stavanger, paving the way for the landing of the main expeditionary force.

May 10 1940 saw the start of the first attempt in history to conquer a country from the air. First the bombers pounded the Dutch airfields, and then 4,000 of Student's paratroops descended, supported by the 22nd Air Landing Division. They occupied the areas around Dordrecht and Moerdijk while further troops were landed by seaplane on the river at Rotterdam. Spreading alarm and confusion, they managed to hold out until relieved by the 8th Panzer Division, which had advanced rapidly from the bridge over the Maas at Gennep – which had been captured by a trick.

Student's greatest single achievement, however, was the capture of the Belgian fort at Eben Emäel, likewise on 10 May. A small force was landed on top of the fort in gliders and succeeded in blowing in the gun turrets with hollow charges.

As a result of these successes Student was much caressed by Goebbel's propaganda machinery. He had been wounded in the fighting at Rotterdam and was forced out of things for several months. However, he was a loyal adherent of Hitler and National Socialism, and as such he was the sort of hero that was required.

In the spring of 1941 he was back in action and able to lead his XI Air Korps in the Balkan campaign. On 3 May 1941 he stood beside Field Marshal List on the saluting base at the victory parade in Athens; but in British eyes he will always be associated with the battles in Crete later in the month. In this operation his corps played the dominant rôle, although the final victory was far from a foregone conclusion. Some of his superiors wanted to call the whole operation off at one stage: all the landings had been bitterly opposed, Student's losses were appalling (nearly 6,500 men), and a number of his senior officers were either killed or wounded. Against his will he was not allowed to land in Crete personally until the danger was less.

Although Student did not know it at the time, Crete was the swansong of the German paratroops. Aircraft were in short supply and were needed in Russia for transport purposes. He spent several frustrating months in 1942 preparing for an airborne invasion of Malta which he tried to 'sell' to Hitler without success. Parachute units continued to expand, but except for a few minor drops they were 'airborne' in name only – paradoxically, at a time when the Allies were getting organised along the lines which Student had developed.

In 1944 Student was commanding the 1st Parachute Army, and one of his protégés, Meindl, led the 11 Parachute Corps in Normandy. After the Allied breakout Student's troops found themselves in the front line in Belgium and Holland, and together with Model he became involved in organising the defence at Arnhem.

Hermann Balck at the height of his career, decorated with the Swords and Oakleaves to the Knight's Cross. He was a man of great physical courage, once leading an attack in person armed with a walking stick, and on another occasion driving among attacking T-34s in his Kübelwagen, complete with command pennant, on the grounds that at close range their poor visibility kept him safe. His moral courage was also notable; he once told the formidable Model that his impulsive interference was unsettling his subordinates, and successfully dissuaded 'the Führer's fireman' from making any more lightning descents on XLVIII Panzer-Korps. (Imp. War Mus.)

In Holland Student displayed tenacity and organisational capability in defending the country with his paratroops and whatever other units he could scrape together. In October he became commander of Army Group H with control over all forces in the north of Holland, but was relieved by Blaskowitz in February 1945. From then until the final surrender he remained in charge of his parachute army, a tough, well-disciplined force.

After the war Kurt Student lived in honourable retirement, and died in 1978 at the age of 82.

Colonel-General Hermann Balck

Balck was one of those soldiers who would have done well in any army at any period in history. He was a rough, tough, fighting man who was a natural in the profession of arms. His rise was meteoric during the Second World War – from lieutenant-colonel to colonel-general, from a regiment to an army group. Although he was popular with Hitler, his promotions were largely due to sheer ability.

He was born in 1895 into an old army family, and was half-English. His great-grandfather had served as a staff officer under Wellington in the Peninsula. Hermann naturally joined the Imperial Army, and as a junior officer served with distinction during the First World War, during the course of which he was five times wounded.

After the war he gravitated into the Reichswehr, and played a part in the development of the German armoured forces. His chance came during the campaign in France in 1940. As a lieutenant-colonel he commanded the 1st Rifle Regiment, which was the motorised infantry component of the 1st Panzer Division. Serving in Guderian's Panzer Group, Balck's infantrymen were among the first across the Meuse at Sedan and then stormed the heights above the river on the west bank. A few days later he was awarded the Knight's Cross in the field, and took command of the 1st Panzer Brigade.

In the summer of 1941, still a colonel, he was again serving under Guderian for the invasion of Russia, having spent the intervening period as a staff officer at Army headquarters (OKH). He then took over the famous 11th Panzer Division, and later commanded the XLVIII Panzer Korps in the desperate battles around Lemberg. As a general of armoured troops, his last command in Russia was the 4th Panzer Army.

In September 1944 Balck left Russia to take over command of Army Group G, replacing the sacked Blaskowitz. His job was to hold Lorraine and stop Patton while preparations for the Ardennes offensive were completed. With low priority in terms of reinforcements, and using a policy of elastic defence, he fulfilled his mission with great skill. Although branded by some as a martinet and an 'incurable optimist', his fighting attitude recommended him to the Führer.

In early 1945 Balck was moved back to the East to command 6th Army in Hungary, where he fought a series of rearguard actions during the retreat back into Austria. His career was in many ways typical of those who as soldiers served the Nazi regime faithfully until the end – without being part of it.

Colonel-General Johannes Blaskowitz

Blaskowitz was described by General Blumentritt as 'a fine soldier' and an 'able leader'. Born in 1878, he was thus one of the oldest and most senior generals in the army. After service with distinction during the First World War and survival during the twilight period of the Reichswehr, by 1935 he was a lieutenant-general in command of a corps. He also survived the 1938 purge, and the following year was promoted to general of infantry.

In the Polish campaign he commanded the 8th Army under von Rundstedt; and on 27 September 1939 he negotiated the surrender of the Poles. Blaskowitz saw nothing wrong with invading Poland, but after the campaign he was made military commander. Horrified by the excesses committed by the Party and the SS, he protested to Brauchitsch, the professional chief of the German army. As a result he was side-tracked for the following four years, missing out on the triumphs in France and Russia.

By 1943 Blaskowitz was commanding an army corps in the occupation of France; he had missed out on the mass promotions, but also steered clear of the bomb plotters. In 1944, however, he was given command of an army group (G), which was responsible for all of France south of the Loire, and when the 'Anvil' landings took place on the Riviera coast his forces bore the brunt. With only two inferior armies, and with his communications hampered by the Resistance, he was forced to retreat. He conducted a fighting withdrawal back to the Vosges and the line of the Moselle, only to be sacked in September after the failure of an armoured counter-attack ordered by Hitler.

During the winter he was employed in organising the defence in the Vosges sector, and in January 1945 he was placed in command of Army Group H, which was holding the front in the Low Countries. This again was hardly a plum job, but

Generalfeldmarschall Friedrich Paulus (1890–1951) photographed as a PoW in Russia after his capture at Stalingrad; note that the Nazi national emblem has been removed from the breast, although rank insignia are retained. He is supposedly signing an appeal by the German Officers' League, part of the National Committee for Free Germany organised by German Communists in the USSR. A very capable Hessian staff officer, Paulus was given to slow and deliberate calculations; had a younger and more impulsive officer been in command, 6th Army might have achieved at least a partial break-out from the Stalingrad encirclement in defiance of Hitler's 'last man, last bullet' orders. Paulus lived in East Germany after the war. (Novosti)

Blaskowitz managed to pull his motley troops together and to organise a bitter resistance to the Allies. He fought to the end in Holland, and was only prepared to consider capitulation when the death of Hitler became known.

After the war he went into captivity and in 1948 he was brought to Nürnberg to await trial as one of the lesser war criminals. In February he committed suicide in prison, although a conviction in his case would have been unlikely. Basically, Blaskowitz was an honest and decent soldier who, had he been given the chance, could well have outshone some of his more illustrious contemporaries.

Lieutenant-General Fritz Bayerlein

Bayerlein, born in 1900, was one of the more junior commanders in the German army, and in post-war interrogations was able to take an objective view of events. During the latter part of the war in Europe he commanded an élite division, but by then most of the scope for individual initiative by commanders had been lost to Hitler.

Bayerlein first came to notice as a colonel with the post of chief-of-staff to the Afrikakorps, firstly under Rommel and then under the later commanders. He took temporary command of the corps at Alam-el-Halfa, but was forced to fight the battle at short notice as his commanding officer, Nehring, had been wounded. At El Alamein his superior was General von Thoma; when the latter was captured Bayerlein again took command of the Afrikakorps. He was withdrawn to Europe before the final surrender in Tunisia, however.

At the outset of the Normandy battle he was a major-general in command of the crack Panzer-Lehr-Division, which had been assembled from various instructional schools and demonstration battalions. In 1944 it had been specifically earmarked for an anti-invasion rôle, and was the best-equipped armoured unit in the German army. At the end of March it was briefly switched to Poland, but by mid-May it was back in the West. Under the energetic leadership of Fritz Bayerlein the division took part in the early battles around Caen; like all the German armoured units it suffered heavily from Allied air superiority – which Bayerlein had learnt to respect in the desert war.

At the end of July the division was almost wiped out as it bore the brunt of the ferocious bombing along the St. Lô-Perriers road as part of Operation 'Cobra'. The remnants took part in the counter-attack at Avranches, and more were lost in the Falaise pocket. After a fighting retreat across the Seine, Bayerlein's division was sent back to Germany to refit for the Ardennes offensive. Replacements, however, were not well trained. With only some 70 tanks, it was thrown in November into the battles along the Saar and the Siegfried Line. In December Bayerlein led his division in the Ardennes as part of the spearhead of von Manteuffel's army. There he missed capturing Bastogne, on account of having lost his way. The division again suffered heavily, but in January he was placed in command of LIII Korps. With this unit he fought on until forced to surrender in the Rühr pocket at the end of March.

After the war he co-operated with the Allied interrogators and in various historical studies.

Field Marshal Fedor von Bock

Von Bock's father was ennobled for bravery by Kaiser Wilhelm I during the Franco-Prussian War, rising to become a major-general. The son, who was to become a field marshal, was born in December 1880 in Küstrin, and after schooling was sent to a cadet academy. From this he passed out as a lieutenant in 1898 into the 5th Regiment of Foot Guards. In 1912, as a captain, he was transferred to the General Staff. During the First World War, except for a brief period as a battalion commander, all von Bock's service was on the staff, for which he was awarded the Pour le Mérite in 1918.

Von Bock was retained in the Army after the war, serving both as a staff officer and a troop commander. In 1925 he was a regimental commander and full colonel, and in 1929 he was promoted to major-general in command of a cavalry division. As a result of the expansion of the Army after the Nazi seizure of power he became a general in command of an army corps and, in 1935, a colonel-general. Von Bock commanded the troops who occupied Austria in 1938 and then took a leading part in the invasion of Czechoslovakia. Towards the end of that year he replaced von Rundstedt in command of the 1st Army Group.

In September 1939 he led two armies to victory in the brief Poland campaign (Heeresgruppe Nord) by breaking through the Polish Corridor into East Prussia, and was then transferred to the Western Front. In the original planning for the attack on France his Army Group B, based on the Dutch and Belgian frontiers, was to make the main effort; but after the adoption of the Manstein plan he lost most of the armoured divisions. Liddell-Hart described his rôle then as a 'matador's cloak' to entice the British and French into Belgium while the armour broke through to the south. Von Bock's troops captured Paris, where he was able to take the salute on the Champs Elysées, and as a reward he was one of the batch of field marshals promoted after the French campaign.

In June 1941 he commanded Army Group

1. Generalmajor Heinz Guderian, 1937
2. Generalfeldmarschall Gerd von Runstedt, 1940
3. Generaloberst Eduard Dietl, 1940

A

B

1. Generalfeldmarschall Erwin Rommel, 1943
2. Oberst Fritz Bayerlein, 1942
3. Generalmajor Bernhard Ramcke, 1942-43

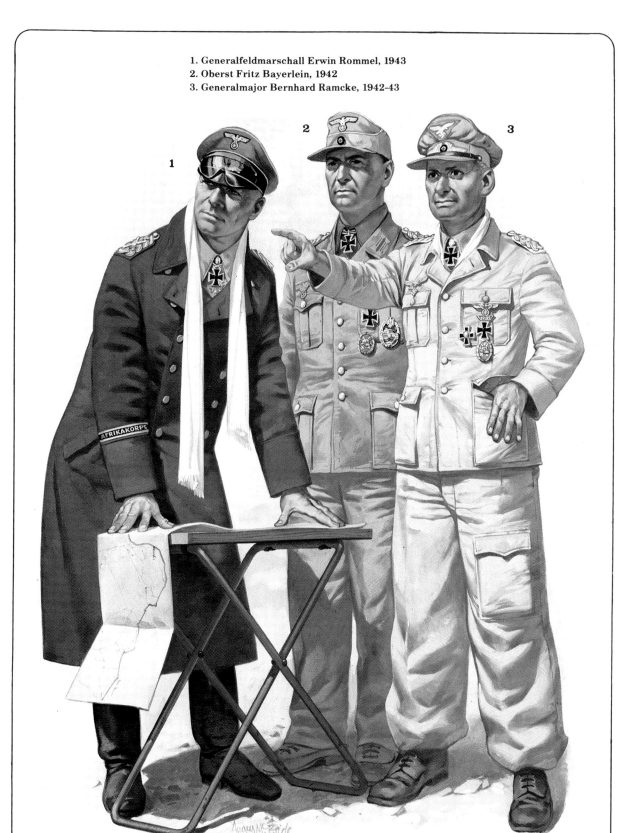

1. Generalfeldmarschall Albert Kesselring, 1942
2. Generalfeldmarschall Wilhelm List, 1941
3. Generaloberst Jürgen von Arnim, 1943

D

1. Generaloberst Walter Model, 1943
2. Generalleutnant Hasso Freiherr von Manteuffel, 1944
3. General der Infanterie Erich von Manstein, 1942

E

1. Generaloberst Ewald von Kleist, 1942
2. SS-Brigadeführer Felix Steiner, 1941
3. Generalfeldmarschall Ferdinand Schörner, 1944

F

1. SS-Obergruppenführer Paul Hausser, 1944
2. Generalleutnant Eugen Meindl, 1944
3. SS-Obergruppenführer 'Sepp' Dietrich, 1944

1. Generaloberst Gotthard Heinrici, 1945
2. Grossadmiral Karl Dönitz, 1944
3. SS-Gruppenführer Hermann Fegelein, 1945

H

Centre for the invasion of Russia and led the victorious advance towards Moscow, but in the autumn was forced by a stomach complaint to take sick leave – just before the Russian counter-offensive. However, in January 1942 he was back as a replacement for von Reichenau in command of Army Group South. Again he led his troops successfully, but in July he was retired after a number of disagreements with Hitler.

This 'most Prussian' of the German generals spent the rest of the war as a pensioner, resisting the blandishments of the resistance movement. By a quirk of fate he was never called upon to justify his conduct to the Allies. In May 1945 he and his wife were killed by a low-flying aircraft while travelling in a car in North Germany.

Field Marshal Ernst Busch

Ernst Busch was born in 1885 into a family with no particular military connections (his father was the director of an orphanage), but he became a cadet in the Prussian army. In 1904 he graduated as a lieutenant in the infantry. At the beginning of the First World War Busch was a company commander, and unlike most of the others examined in this book he spent the whole period of the war as a field commander. He participated in most of the main actions on the Western Front, and was awarded the Pour la Mérite as a battalion commander.

After the war it took him until 1925 to gain the rank of major in the Reichswehr, and until 1930 to become a battalion commander once again. By 1937 he was a lieutenant-general commanding a division, and, being completely uninterested in politics, he profited from the purge in February 1938, being promoted to general of infantry and being given command of a corps. In the process he advanced above many others with greater seniority.

Busch led his corps in Poland with distinction and was popular with his men, perhaps as a result of his First World War experience. In France in the spring and summer of 1940 he commanded the 16th Army on the left wing of von Rundstedt's Army Group A, and managed to capture Verdun in a matter of hours. At the close of the French campaign he was awarded the Ritterkreuz and promoted to colonel-general.

Ernst Busch wearing medals for physical courage earned in two World Wars; sadly, it seems that his moral courage was of a less impressive order. He obeyed patently absurd 'no retreat' orders from OKW; and when in June 1944 his 34 divisions were swamped by 200 Soviet divisions he tried to compel the commander of 4th Army, Tippelskirch, to counter-attack after that able and experienced officer had used his initiative to withdraw the shattered remnant of his troops across the Dniepr. His reputation preceded him to the West, where even junior subordinates tended to regard his orders with extreme cynicism. (Imp. War Mus.)

During 1941 and 1942 his army fought on the Baltic front, and although Busch did not necessarily agree with Hitler he was not the man to contradict his superior. His reward for this loyalty was promotion to field marshal in February 1943, and command in November of the central group of armies. In this capacity he was over-promoted, and although always obedient to Hitler's will, he was unable to hinder the Russian breakthrough in the summer of 1944. In June he was sacked and replaced by Model.

In the last few weeks of the war Busch was

recalled and made commander of all the troops still fighting in the West, far too late to be able to alter the situation. Thus he was fated to preside over the final surrender to Montgomery, but was left for a while in command of the remaining German units in North Germany.

Finally, Ernst Busch was brought as a prisoner to Aldershot, England, where he died of a heart ailment in June 1945. He was a good leader of troops in the field, and a plain soldier who avoided political involvement. His tragedy was that the Nazi regime brought him promotion beyond his capabilities.

Field Marshal Ewald von Kleist

There have been three field marshals who bore the name von Kleist, and in the Prussian army list of 1913 there were 44 officers of that name. Ewald von Kleist came from an academic family, however, and was born in August 1881. In 1900 he joined the field artillery as a cadet, rising to the rank of captain just before the outbreak of the First World War and transferring to the cavalry.

During the war he took part in the Battle of Tannenberg, and later joined the General Staff on the Western Front. After the collapse of Germany Captain von Kleist joined one of the many Freikorps before being accepted into the small professional army that remained under the provisions of the Treaty of Versailles, the Reichswehr. During the period of the Weimar Republic he served both as a troop commander and a staff officer, rising to the rank of major-general before Hitler came to power.

This event brought him promotion to lieutenant-general in October 1933, and command of the 8th Division stationed at Breslau in Silesia. While there he became embroiled with local Nazi Party officials and made himself very unpopular, refusing to socialise with SA officers. In 1936 he was again promoted, to general of cavalry, and was given command of a corps; but in February 1938 he was retired along with many other senior officers as a result of the Blomberg-Fritsch purge. War, however, brought about von Kleist's re-instatement, and as commander of the XXII (Motorised) Korps he took part in the Polish campaign.

It was in France that von Kleist first acquired

Ewald von Kleist received the Swords to his Knight's Cross in March 1944, as sweetening for the bitter pill of dismissal from command of Army Group A, which he had saved from encirclement in the Caucasus and withdrawn through the narrow Rostov corridor in January–March 1944. This withdrawal was marred by the failure to extricate the Crimean garrison, which lost 26,700 out of 64,700 men. Von Kleist was highly regarded by his colleagues for his old-fashioned virtues and unflappable control in attack and retreat alike. (Imp. War Mus.)

prominence. He commanded the Panzergruppe Kleist which comprised all except two of the German armoured formations plus three motorised infantry divisions. At the time this was the largest mechanised formation that had ever been used in war; and although Guderian and Rommel are always associated with the breakthrough in May 1940, Kleist was in overall charge. His reward was promotion to colonel-general.

His next campaign was in the Balkans in early 1941, where his Panzer group led the fighting in Yugoslavia and Greece, before being transferred to the Russian frontier. Like many of the German generals, it was in Russia that von Kleist made his reputation. In the initial attack in the summer of

Of the same generation as von Rundstedt, Wilhelm Ritter von Leeb was described at his post-war trial as 'no friend or follower of the Nazi Party'. It seems that his heart was not in the war from the first, and he had to be dissuaded from refusing to take part in the invasion of France. The failure to take Leningrad can be laid jointly at his feet and those of his Führer – whose meddling prompted him to remark that Hitler and Stalin seemed to be allies. His strong religious and moral convictions led him to the unenviable position of being the first general to be put under Gestapo surveillance; however, he was not involved in the assassination plots, and somewhat miraculously survived the war. (Imp. War Mus.)

1941 he led his tanks to the south of the Pripet Marshes and by the end of the year he was commanding 1. Panzerarmee. At the end of 1942 he replaced List in command of Army Group A, and in February 1943 he was made a field marshal.

In early 1944, together with von Manstein, Kleist was sacked and took no further part in the war. In October 1954 he died in a Russian prison camp.

Field Marshal Wilhelm Ritter von Leeb

The title Ritter can be equated with a knighthood, and was granted by the King of Bavaria to those who were awarded the Max-Joseph Order. Wilhelm Leeb was born on 5 September 1876 in Landsberg in Bavaria, and in 1895 he joined a Bavarian field artillery regiment as a cadet. In 1900, as a volunteer, he took part in the suppression of the Boxer uprising in China. After the usual round of appointments and courses Captain Leeb joined the Bavarian General Staff before the First World War, and served throughout the whole period of hostilities as a staff officer. This brought him the above-mentioned award and promotion to major.

Between the wars Ritter von Leeb, having become a Bavarian nobleman, served in the Reichswehr, becoming a colonel in 1925 and a lieutenant-general in 1930. Thus when Hitler came to power von Leeb was already a senior general, and during the early 1930s he made a considerable contribution to the rebuilding of the German Army. He helped to found the mountain troops, and wrote a number of studies on defensive strategy and tactics.

Von Leeb, however, as a sincerely religious man, did not fit into the Nazi pattern, and was required to resign in early 1938 together with a large number of other senior officers. He was temporarily 're-activated' in the autumn of 1938 in connection with the occupation of the Sudetenland, and as an army commander he took part in the march into the rest of Czechoslovakia in March 1939.

When the war broke out von Leeb was officially re-instated in the Army as a colonel-general, and as commander of Army Group C was made responsible for holding the Western Front during the invasion of Poland. In May 1940 his army group continued on the defensive, but in June was able to break through the thinly-held Maginot Line. In July he was one of the group of generals promoted to field marshal.

For the attack on Russia in the summer of 1941 von Leeb was given command of the northern group of armies. His troops advanced rapidly towards Leningrad, but were then stopped on Hitler's order. Condemned to dig-in through the Russian winter, their morale suffered, and von Leeb asked to be relieved.

After January 1942 he was never re-employed and lived in retirement in Bavaria, where he was captured by American troops in 1945. Von Leeb was tried as a war criminal with other German generals, and was sentenced to five years' imprisonment. He was soon released, and died in April 1956 aged almost 80.

Field Marshal Wilhelm List

List was one of the oldest generals to serve in the German Army during the Second World War; like his colleague von Bock he was born in 1880. The son of a doctor, he attended school in Munich and in 1898 he joined the Bavarian army as a cadet, passing out as a lieutenant in 1900. Before the First World War he went through the various stages of staff training and in 1913 joined the General Staff as a captain. He served right through until 1918 as a staff officer, was wounded, and was awarded a number of decorations.

Experienced staff officers were welcome in the post-war Reichswehr, and except for a short period as a battalion commander most of List's

Wilhelm List photographed during 1937 manoeuvres – note the tell-tale white cap-bands in the background, identifying umpires. His service in eastern Europe in the First World War led to his appointment to command the invasion of Yugoslavia and Greece in 1941 after considerable successes in France. A diplomatist as well as a general, List was highly regarded by Rommel. (Imp. War Mus.)

service in the 1920s and early '30s was spent as an administrator. He was promoted to colonel in 1927, major-general in 1930 and lieutenant-general in 1932. The following year he was in command of 4th Division in Saxony, which was then expanded into a corps in 1935. List, as general of infantry, remained in command.

Politically neutral, he survived the purge of early 1938 and was made responsible for integrating the Austrian Army into the Wehrmacht. When war broke out List commanded the 14th Army in Poland, which brought him the Knight's Cross. In France, again under von Rundstedt, he commanded the 12th Army in the breakthrough at Sedan, and later in the long march to the Swiss frontier. His contribution to the defeat of France was considerable and he was rewarded with his marshal's baton in the general rash of promotions in July 1940.

Still in command of the 12th Army, List next appears in the Balkans in early 1941. Together with Student's paratroops and Schörner's mountain division, he was largely responsible for the conquest of Greece and the expulsion of the British from Salonika, and after the reduction of Crete he took over as Supreme Commander South East.

In July 1942 he was moved to Russia to command Army Group A, the mission of which was to advance into the Caucasus to seize the oilfields. List was a careful planner rather than a 'blitzkrieg' enthusiast, and his command only lasted a couple of months. By refusing to commit his exhausted troops to a further operation he drew upon himself the wrath of Hitler, and was sacked in September.

Wilhelm List thus joined the unemployed list for the rest of the war. Afterwards he was charged as a war criminal and sentenced to life imprisonment for actions against partisans in the Balkans. After serving eight years he was released in 1953, and finally died in August 1971 at the ripe old age of 91.

Field Marshal Ferdinand Schörner

Schörner was the last of Hitler's army field marshals, and one of the most controversial. He was born in June 1892 in Munich, the son of a police officer, and when he left school in 1911 he

The hatchet face of Ferdinand Schörner can be seen on the right, beyond Marshal Antonescu, the Rumanian national leader. Among German generals Schörner stands unique as the one man Hitler held in awe. Though very harsh on rear echelon troops, he sometimes deliberately disobeyed Hitler's orders if they meant needless front-line losses. He was a coarse, vulgar man, who boasted a Gold Party Badge as an early member of the NSDAP; and in Russia his ruthlessness matched that of the enemy he faced. Though deprived of a pension after his release from prison in the 1950s, he received monthly cheques of equivalent value from a voluntary collection among veterans of the 6th Mountain Division which he had commanded in the Balkans and Russia. (Imp. War Mus.)

served as a volunteer for a year in the Bavarian Army. After this he settled down to study philosophy and modern languages with a view to becoming a schoolmaster. His academic career was cut short by the outbreak of the First World War, however, most of which he spent as a lieutenant and company commander. In spite of the humble rank, the reservist Schörner covered himself with glory, earning both Iron Crosses and the Pour le Mérite, as well as a reputation for toughness.

In the chaotic period at the end of the war Schörner served in the famous Freikorps led by Ritter von Epp, fighting Communists before being accepted into the Reichswehr. In the 1920s he qualified for the General Staff, and in 1931 he became an instructor in tactics and military history at the Infantry School in Dresden. In 1937 he was promoted to lieutenant-colonel in command of the 98th Mountain Regiment, and it was with this type of troops that he was to make his name.

He fought brilliantly with his regiment in

Poland and in the early stages of the campaign in the West, and at the end of May 1940 he took command of the 6th Mountain Division. As a major-general he led his division in Greece, always well up in front and driving his men unmercifully. 'Sweat saves Blood' was one of his favourite sayings.

Throughout the bitter fighting in Russia Schörner rose steadily in rank, always being sent where there was trouble. As a convinced National Socialist he had no conflict with his conscience to trouble him, and won the Knight's Cross in all its grades. In early 1945 Colonel-General Schörner was given command of the central group of armies, which was in the process of collapse. He managed to stabilise the front and fought a series of delaying actions against the Russians. In April 1945 he was promoted to field marshal, and ended up as a prisoner of the Americans. They handed him over to the Russians, who tried him and sentenced him to 25 years' imprisonment. He was repatriated in 1955, but then had to face charges of manslaughter before a West German court. After two further years in prison Hitler's last field marshal died of a heart attack in July 1973. The Russian Marshal Koniev once wrote: 'If it had not been for Schörner, the Red Army would have marched right through to Bavaria.'

Field Marshal Erwin von Witzleben

The son of a captain in a Prussian Guard regiment, Erwin von Witzleben was born in 1881 into a well-known military family. After the usual training as a cadet he entered the Army as a lieutenant in the summer of 1901, being posted to a grenadier regiment stationed in Silesia. By 1914 he had risen to captain, and served in the trenches as a company and then a battalion commander in an infantry regiment. He fought in Flanders and at Verdun, and after being severely wounded went for General Staff training in 1918.

Von Witzleben ended the war highly decorated but still a substantive captain. He took part in the Freikorps fighting on the Polish frontier; in 1923 he was promoted to major in the Reichswehr, serving on the staff of a division, and by 1931 he had reached the rank of colonel in command of an infantry regiment.

A committed anti-Nazi before the war, von Witzleben was nearly instrumental in launching a coup against Hitler in 1938. As C-in-C France he built up a staff of subordinates of similar convictions, and after retirement due to ill health he was implicated in the July Plot. He was to suffer the same hideous fate as other leaders of the resistance; Gestapo interrogation, an infamous 'show trial' during which he was mocked and goaded by the repulsive Judge Freisler, and death by hanging in a noose of thin wire, his final struggles being filmed for Hitler's pleasure. (Imp. War Mus.)

The decisive point in von Witzleben's career came with the Nazi take-over in 1933. On the surface he achieved rapid promotion – major-general in early 1934, lieutenant-general in 1935 and general of infantry in the following year. He was, however, one of the earliest members of the military resistance group centred around Colonel-General Ludwig Beck, and was party to a number of the plots to kill Hitler.

The latter's string of bloodless victories in Austria and Czechoslovakia tended to cut the ground from under the feet of the plotters. Von Witzleben was not sacked in the army purge of February 1938, but he was transferred away from Berlin. In 1939 he was again promoted, to colonel-general, and when war broke out he commanded the 1st Army. This was initially in a holding position in the West, but in June 1940 von Witzleben took his army through the Magi-

not Line. As a reward he was one of the initial group of promotions to field marshal.

At the close of the campaign in France von Witzleben was appointed as supreme commander in the West (OB West), but in early 1943 he retired on account of ill-health.

During his retirement he kept in touch with the Resistance movement, and was foreseen as the head of all German armed forces in the event of a coup. When the bomb exploded on 20 June 1944 in Hitler's HQ in East Prussia von Witzleben was in Berlin ready to take charge. Arrested a few days later, he was expelled in dishonour from the Army and handed over to the Gestapo, eventually to be sentenced to death by the notorious People's Court. In August 1944 he was hanged with piano wire, the highest-ranking officer to be executed as a result of the plot.

The Plates

Uniform research by Martin Windrow, Graham Scott and William Fowler.

A1: Generalmajor Heinz Guderian, 1937

Only one published photo shows Guderian wearing the special black vehicle uniform of the Panzer arm which he did so much to create and to lead to triumph. It was taken during the 1937 summer manoeuvres of 2. Panzer-Division, the formation Guderian commanded at that date. The padded crash-cap is covered with black cloth and with a black beret; normally the insignia were in silver machine-weaving, and as the insignia of the general officer's service cap were silver at this date it is fair to assume that Guderian did not wear a special gold set. The national eagle on the right breast of the jacket would, however, be in gold wire. The pink-piped death's-head collar patches were worn by all ranks of the Panzerwaffe including generals. Over this uniform Guderian wears the general's field grey gabardine greatcoat with dark green collar and bright red lapel facings; this has gold buttons, and normal shoulder straps of rank in gold and silver cord on the red backing of general officers.

Guderian in his command half-track in France, 1940. Forbidden by Hitler to advance any further at one point in this campaign, he simply left his radio rear-link behind and pushed on, using a telephone to link himself to the static headquarters. After Dunkirk his sweeping left hook to roll up French forces facing the German border – almost a complete reversal of his axis of advance – showed the very high standard of command and control which he had instilled into his Panzer Divisions.

A2: Generalfeldmarschall Gerd von Rundstedt, early 1940

The doyen of the field marshals wears the regulation *Schirmmütze* – service cap – for general officers, with gold piping and cords but silver insignia. His pre-war service tunic has seven gold buttons and slash side pockets; the breeches have the general officer's red stripes and piping down the outer seams, and are worn with polished top-boots. Unusual features particularly associated with von Rundstedt's uniforms are the white (infantry) piping down the front of the tunic; and the use of the full-dress collar patches – *Doppellitzen* – from the 'uniform tunic' or *Rock* of an infantry officer, in silver on white backing. His shoulder straps were also non-regulation, being made with white backing and bearing the gilt '18' of 18. Infanterie-Regiment. He was proud of his special appointment as *Chef* or colonel-in-chief of this unit, and the non-regulation features of his tunic all proclaimed the fact. The full-dress version of the marshal's baton is carried here; the shaft was covered with red

material studded with rows of alternating 'armed forces' eagles, Iron Crosses and Greek crosses.

A3: Generaloberst Eduard Dietl, July 1940

In this month the hero of Narvik received the very first award of the Oakleaves to the Knight's Cross. Photos show him in this piped version of the service tunic – note the red of the general officer's insignia backing used as piping at collar, front and cuffs. The mountain troops' cap bears gold buttons, and the Edelweiss arm-of-service badge on the side, but not at this date crown-piping for commissioned ranks. The puttees and

Generaloberst Eduard Dietl was a Bavarian officer with a considerable experience of mountain warfare. After the near-victory at Narvik in 1940 he was highly decorated, and given great propaganda exposure by Goebbels, who described him as '. . . a true People's General . . . constantly with his troops, and has achieved a popularity which is indescribable.' His divisional command in Norway was expanded to a corps for the invasion of Russia, and entrusted with the defence of the Arctic left flank and the capture of Murmansk, the main port for the Allied supply convoys to the USSR. He failed to reach Murmansk, or to cut its rail links effectively. Killed in an air crash in summer 1944, he was remembered with affection not only by the men of 20th Mountain Army but by the Finns as well. (Imp. War Mus.)

heavily-cleated mountain boots were not uncommon among officers of this arm. Decorations on the chest include the 1914 Iron Cross, and the small silver eagle 'bar' marking a subsequent Second World War award; the silver Wound Badge, for three or four wounds; and, on the right pocket, the rare and prized Mountain Guide's Badge. Dietl does not seem to have qualified for this, so it was probably an honorary award. Generals wore gold eagle insignia on the

Born in Austria in 1889, the distinctively bearded Generalleutnant Julius Ringel (left, decorating an officer in Crete) took command of 5th Mountain Division in time for the Balkan and Crete campaigns of 1941. The intervention of his division in support of the airborne landings clinched the victory on Crete; he later commanded mountain formations around Lake Ladoga on the northern Russian front, and around Cassino in Italy. 'Papa Julius' used to joke about his advanced age, saying that he had received rank and decorations simply by living so long, but was an effective and popular commander. He used to tell a wry anecdote deflating the pretensions to widespread fame of military commanders. Once on the Leningrad front one of his fellow Austrians in his command failed to recognise his divisional commander. In a fairly gentle hint, Ringel pointed to his Knight's Cross and asked the soldier what he thought *that* was; the man replied, 'Ah – are you perhaps our new padre?'

Generalmajor Adolf Galland, Germany's most famous surviving fighter leader, was born in Westphalia in 1912. He learned much during a combat tour in Spain with the Condor Legion fighter squadron, and applied the lessons in action as a squadron and wing commander in Poland, France and the Battle of Britain, rising rapidly to the rank of lieutenant-colonel and the command of the nine-squadron fighter group JG 26 'Schlageter'. He was named Inspector of the Fighter Arm in November 1941; the post carried the rank of major-general, making Galland, at 29, the youngest German general of modern times. He was a dogged champion of the interests of the combat aircrew, and a strategic realist; eventually his stubborn advocacy of the development of the Me262 jet as an interceptor fighter rather than as a vain-glorious 'attack' aircraft led to his dismissal. He ended the war flying in combat with other surviving aces in the crack jet fighter squadron JV44, and had a total of 104 credited kills. He survived to become a popular figure in the post-war aviation industry. Late in the war photos show a growing fashion for closing the collar of the Luftwaffe officer's four-pocket tunic to the throat, as here. (Imp. War Mus.)

breast, but silver – like all other officers – on the cap.

B1: Oberstleutnant Adolf Galland, autumn 1940
Based on a photo taken while Galland still commanded Jagdgeschwader 26 'Schlageter' on the Channel Coast, about a year before the death of his friend Mölders elevated him to the rank of Generalmajor and the post of Inspector-General of Fighters. The Luftwaffe *Schirmmütze* has the slightly battered appearance beloved of pilots of all nations. For interest we show Galland wearing a captured Royal Air Force flying outfit of Irvin design, which he apparently favoured for cold-weather flying at this date. The cigar was a personal trademark; he had a cigar-lighter fitted in the cockpit of his Bf 109! The flying boots are Luftwaffe issue.

B2: Generaloberst Wolfram Freiherr von Richthofen,
  1941–42
Perhaps the most able of all Luftwaffe commanders, this cousin and former squadron-mate of 'the Red Baron' made a great reputation as a leader of close-support aircraft. He was dashing

and aggressive, specialising in directing the Stukas of his VIII Air Corps in close liaison with leading tank elements – a skill perfected in Spain, in France in 1940, in the Mediterranean and in Russia. In summer 1942 he was given 4th Air Fleet, totalling 39 Gruppen of fighters, bombers and Stukas, and supported Army Group South in the Don offensive. We take this painting from a colour snapshot taken when he landed his Fi 156 Storch to confer with 6. Panzer-Division. He wears the Luftwaffe *Schirmmütze*, which for generals had gold insignia and fittings; the fly-fronted *Fliegerbluse*, piped gold at the collar, with the white-backed shoulder straps and beautiful gold-on-white collar patches of his rank; and white-striped Luftwaffe general's breeches. A very rare decoration is worn on the right sleeve – the commemorative cuff title of Manfred von Richthofen's First World War 'flying circus' in dark blue with silver lettering in two lines: 'Jagdgeschwader Frhr.v. Richthofen Nr.1 1917/18'.

A typical snapshot of Rommel, snatching a hasty meal in his command car, well forward with his front-line tanks. Recent commentators who have correctly pointed out the limitations of this perhaps over-eulogised general cannot detract from his genuinely impressive achievements and attractive character. He was worshipped by his men, and frequently displayed great physical courage.

B3: Generaloberst Alexander Löhr, 1943–44

Head of the Austrian air force before the Anschluss, Löhr held senior commands in the Polish campaign of 1939 and in the invasion of Crete, 1941, before leading the air support for Army Group South in the invasion of Russia. In 1942 he became C-in-C Balkans; he was air commander in Italy, January–August 1943, and then became C-in-C Greece, the Aegean and Yugoslavia – both of the Air Force and the Army occupation troops. He was thus the only Air Force general apart from Kesselring to hold a theatre command. He was unlucky enough to be captured by the partisans in the last months of the war; held responsible for atrocities committed under his command, he was hanged.

He wears the regulation Luftwaffe general's service uniform of four-pocket tunic and white-striped breeches, with a gold-furnished cap. Among his decorations are the *Krimschild*, awarded for service in the Crimea 1941–42, on the left upper arm; and the *Kreta* cuff title on the left forearm, for the invasion of Crete. The pilot/observer's badge on the left breast is the gold and diamond version awarded by Göring to a favoured few.

C1: Generalfeldmarschall Erwin Rommel, 1943

Based on a colour photo apparently taken in Tunisia, this outfit differs from the leather greatcoat and goggled *Schirmmütze* more usually illustrated. The headgear is the 'old style officer's field cap' with gold piping and silver machine-woven insignia, worn here with the habitual British gas-goggles. The brown tropical greatcoat worn in the photo definitely has the red lapel facings of a general, although other sources have denied that these were applied to this coat. It has the usual shoulder straps of rank, gold buttons, and the 'Afrikakorps' cuff title. Rommel habitually wore both the Knight's Cross (by this date, with Oakleaves and Swords) and the 'Blue Max' which he won at the Isonzo in the First World War, hanging one above the other at the throat. The white evening scarf is not seen in many photos – his famous wool check was more typical.

C2: Oberst Fritz Bayerlein, 1942

Taken from a photo showing Bayerlein as Rommel's chief-of-staff in the desert. His faded or bleached officer's version of the tropical field cap has silver piping and insignia. The tunic and long trousers are of normal issue style, in faded olive-khaki. The tunic still bears the enlisted man's collar *Litzen* and breast eagle in pale blue on brown – many officers did not bother to substitute their own insignia. As a Panzer colonel Bayerlein wears shoulder straps of rank on pink *Waffenfarbe* backing. His decorations include the

Knight's Cross, the Iron Cross 1st Class, a Tank Battle Badge and the silver class of the Wound Badge.

C3: Generalmajor Bernhard Ramcke, 1942–43
The renowned commander of paratroopers in North Africa, from a famous photograph. He wears the tropical service cap issued to Luftwaffe field personnel, the 'Meyer' cap – note long peak and unstiffened crown, with white machine-woven insignia and leather strap. The Luftwaffe-issue tropical uniform, in pale yellowish-khaki drill, contrasted in both colour and cut with the Army equivalent. Shoulder straps were worn,

Generalfeldmarschall Walther von Brauchitsch (1881–1948) was C-in-C of the German Army until replaced in December 1941 after the successful Russian counter-attack before Moscow. Between the wars he had played an important rôle in the adoption of the 88mm anti-aircraft gun for anti-tank use. No friend of the Nazis, he was not equal to the task of standing up to Hitler, and lost credibility as an independent professional leader of the officer corps.

but no collar patches; and note pin-on breast eagle, here in general officer's gold finish. The decorations are all conventional apart from the rather obscure cross worn left of the Iron Cross 1st Class: this may be the Prussian Military Service Cross which he won as a young marine fighting the British in Flanders in the First World War.

D1: Generalfeldmarschall Albert Kesselring, August 1942
'Smiling Albert', photographed arriving at a desert airstrip on one of his many visits to Rommel in his capacity as C-in-C South, wears the Luftwaffe tropical uniform with the white-topped summer version of the general's service cap: note that this lacks gold piping at the crown seam. His insignia are hidden by the aircrew lifejacket worn on the flight, but he carries the *Interimstab*: this was the undress version of the marshal's baton, which had a long tricolour cord and tassel attached below the head.

D2: Generalfeldmarschall List, 1941
Photographed in Greece as Supreme Commander South-East, List wears a colourful combination of items. The sun helmet is in the faded olive finish normal for this headgear, and has the

Generaloberst Ritter von Schobert (left, with GFM von Brauchitsch) commanded 11th Army, whose mission in September 1941 was the capture of the Crimea. A Bavarian aristocrat and a convinced Nazi, von Schobert became the first army commander to be killed in action when his Fieseler Storch came down in a Russian minefield; he had previously led VII Korps during the Polish and French campaigns, and it had been selected for the invasion of England – going so far as to adopt rather prematurely a new march, 'England zerkrache!' – 'England, crack open!' On his death 11th Army passed to the brilliant von Manstein.

A stony-faced von Arnim, followed by his chief-of-staff Gen. Kramer, surrenders the Axis forces in North Africa to the Allies, May 1943. Born in 1889, this scion of a traditional Prussian family made his name as commander of 17th Panzer Division in Russia in 1941, and later led XXXIX Panzer Korps in the relief of the Kholm pocket, cut off for three months. Posted to Africa, he did not work well with Rommel, by now a sick and exhausted man. (Personality Picture Library)

normal pinned escutcheons on each side; it seems to differ in small details from the enlisted men's version, and has a false *paggri* effect. The 'new style' officer's white summer tunic has patch side pockets and a fall collar worn without ranking patches: note pin-on eagle. It is worn with the standard red-striped field grey breeches.

D3: Generaloberst Jürgen von Arnim, May 1943

Photographed in the uniform in which he surrendered in Tunisia, Arnim presents a slightly eccentric outline. His conventional *Schirmmütze* was habitually worn in this fiercely stiffened 'boat' shape; and rather than long boots he wore long wool socks and ankle-boots. General officers in Africa wore personally tailored uniforms of a variety of olive and brown shades, following the general cut of the issue tunic, with patches of rank on the open collar; the breeches were not striped. Arnim's decorations are limited here to his *Ritterkreuz,* and a length of Winter 1941–42 Medal ribbon in the buttonhole. The bamboo cane, and a black or dark grey-green leather greatcoat, appear in some photos of his surrender and subsequent journey to Britain.

E1: Generaloberst Walter Model, 1943

Photographed as commander of the 9th Army in Russia, the 'Führer's fireman' wears a *Schirmmütze* with the cords and buttons removed for field use, and the leather greatcoat often privately acquired by German officers. The only insignia applied to this were the shoulder straps of rank. The lapel is worn folded back to display the Knight's Cross worn at the throat of the tunic – Model added the Swords to his *Ritterkreuz mit Eichenlaub* on 2 April 1943.

E2: Generalleutnant Hasso Freiherr von Manteuffel, August 1944

This famous tank general is shown as he appeared in his final month as commander of Panzer-Division 'Grossdeutschland', just before his appointment to 5. Panzer-Armee. His 'old style'

The unmistakable vulpine features of Generaloberst Rudolf Schmidt, the tank general who led 1st Panzer Division and later XXXIV Panzer Korps in Holland, France and Russia, where he served with distinction under Hoth. He was given 2nd Panzer Army after Guderian's dismissal just after Christmas 1941, and fought a series of successful battles around Orel and Bryansk in 1942. He was, in private, an outspoken critic of the Nazis, and was dismissed in 1943 following his brother's arrest by the Gestapo and the discovery of letters from the general.

sional cuff titles and wore them as shown, although the 'Afrika' should officially have been worn on the left sleeve. The gold 'GD' divisional monogram was pinned to his shoulder straps of rank. The gold breast eagle is on Panzer-black backing.

E3: General der Infanterie Erich von Manstein, 1942
The conqueror of the Crimea photographed as commander of 11th Army. He wears a field grey sidecap – *Feldmütze* – with gold piping. His uniform is absolutely regulation for his rank, and rather plain. Photos taken later in the war show him wearing a service tunic with a field grey collar, and gold cap insignia. He has a version of the Iron Cross 1st Class with the 1939 bar actually welded to the top. He sometimes wore the cross of the Rumanian Order of Michael the Victor 2nd Class suspended below his Knight's Cross.

General of Armoured Troops Hasso von Manteuffel (left), the charismatic commander of the 'Grossdeutschland' Division, known as 'the Lion of Zhitomir' after fighting around that town in 1943. A member of one of the oldest Prussian military families, this bantam of a general was renowned for his politeness to subordinates: this extended, during one Russian air attack, to standing aside as his staff leapt into a slit-trench, with the words 'After you, gentlemen!' He twice used the risky tactics of launching major assaults without artillery preparation for the sake of surprise – a ruse which worked well both in the East and the Ardennes, where his forces made the most successful thrust in December 1944.

field cap has gold piping and, apparently, gold insignia – this was authorised for generals on 1 January 1943, but they were ordered not to wear it until after the war, an order quite frequently ignored. His service tunic is slightly unusual in having straight pocket flaps and no box pleats; in field grey, it is worn with striped breeches in contrasting 'new grey'. Cases of two cuff titles being worn on one sleeve are not common; von Manteuffel was entitled to the 'Afrika' campaign and 'Grossdeutschland' divi-

Erich von Manstein (left) with Oberst von Choltitz, who commanded the infantry regiment which was instrumental in breaking into the Sevastopol defences in summer 1942. Promoted field marshal for his success in the Crimea, von Manstein has enjoyed perhaps the highest reputation of any German general. It was said of him that he experienced with equally impressive grasp the three classic phases of war: attack, siege, and retreat. Von Choltitz later became commandant of Paris, and refused to obey Hitler's order to demolish the Seine bridges and burn the city to the ground. Twenty years later a French magazine invited him back to the city he had refused to destroy. (Imp. War Mus.)

Ewald von Kleist, wearing the fur-collared greatcoat illustrated in Plate F1.

wore. He wears a popular front-line alternative to the greatcoat: the rubberised motorcyclist's coat, with a field grey cloth collar. The collar insignia of this rank were changed at the end of this year.

F3: Generalfeldmarschall Ferdinand Schörner, 1944
This grim commander wears, like so many generals towards the end of the war, a gold-furnished version of the 1943 *Einheitsfeldmütze*.

SS-Obergruppenführer und General der Waffen-SS Felix Steiner (1896–1966) was one of the most able of the SS generals. He had served on both Eastern and Western Fronts in 1914–18, including operations in Kurland, where he was to fight again in 1944–45. He resigned from the Army after the First World War, joining the SS-Verfügungstruppe in 1930 and fighting the BEF in France in 1940. His 5th SS Division 'Wiking' penetrated as far as the Maikop oilfields in the Caucasus in 1942, and he was apparently an inspiring commander of the foreign volunteer SS formations of III SS Panzer Korps, decimated at Narva on the Baltic in 1944. By the end of the war he commanded the new 11th Army, which in fact had only divisional strength; disobeying Hitler's hysterical order that he relieve Berlin, he led his men into American captivity. (Imp. War Mus.)

F1: Generaloberst Ewald von Kleist, 1942
Photographed in February on the Russian Front, the Panzergruppe commander wears a large fur cap and has the collar of his general's greatcoat faced with thick fur. It is also unusual in displaying his unique personal shoulder straps. Like von Rundstedt, this cavalry veteran of Tannenberg took great pride in an honorary regimental appointment, in his case to the 8. Kavallerie-Regiment. His shoulder straps of rank bear the gilt regimental number, and are made on cavalry-yellow backing.

F2: SS-Brigadeführer Felix Steiner, late 1941
From photos of the commander of the then SS-Division 'Wiking' early in its eventful career on the Russian Front. SS-Brigaf. Steiner wears the regulation service cap of a Waffen-SS general in field grey with black velvet band and silver piping, silver eagle and death's-head insignia being pinned to crown and band but here somewhat obscured by the goggles he habitually

SS-Obergruppenführer und General der Waffen-SS Joseph Dietrich, wearing normal field grey service uniform and the special gold-piped service cap unique to him; note the Army-style silver-on-green eagle badge on the crown, and compare with the slightly different cap on Plate G3.

His personally-acquired pale sheepskin coat has on the left upper arm the patch of this rank according to the sequence of insignia introduced to the Army in mid-1942 for wear on all clothing not displaying shoulder straps.

G1: SS-Obergruppenführer Paul Hausser, June 1944
The commander of II SS-Panzer-Korps was photographed in Normandy wearing this outfit at a meeting with Rommel and Meindl shortly before D-Day. The field grey *Einheitsfeldmütze* has silver officer's piping; an Army-style woven eagle; and a pinned SS death's-head. The four-pocket tunic of W-SS camouflage material is typical of the type of rather superior combat clothing often privately ordered by officers; he ignores regulations in displaying shoulder straps of rank, on the W-SS general's usual pale grey backing. His plain, unstriped breeches and

service belt with a holstered Walther on his right side underline the front-line nature of this uniform.

G2: Generalleutnant Eugen Meindl, June 1944
This officer commanded II Fallschirm-Korps (3. and 5. Fallschirm-Division) in Normandy and during the subsequent retreat, with considerable distinction. He was promoted full general during the campaign. This is the outfit he wears in photos showing the above-mentioned meeting with Hausser and Rommel. Eccentrically, he has added gold cap cords to his gold-furnished Luftwaffe general's *Einheitsfeldmütze*; and on the left side is a small oval pin, apparently a formation badge, in the shape of what appears to be a winged Gothic M. His faded old first-pattern olive parachute jump-smock bears the Luftwaffe breast eagle in gold, and on both upper arms his rank patch in the Luftwaffe sequence of 'eagles' and bars – for a general, in yellow cloth. His parachutist's trousers have the familiar seam-pocket for the gravity knife; he wears normal laced ankle-boots rather than the old-pattern side-laced jump-boots.

G3: SS-Obergruppenführer 'Sepp' Dietrich, April 1944
The commander of I SS-Panzer-Korps 'Leibstandarte Adolf Hitler' had a fondness for personal uniform flourishes. This painting is taken from a photo of Dietrich at Thouars, France, on 10 April, attending the naming ceremony for the new SS division 'Götz von Berlichingen'. His hat was unique for an SS general; it was made from an Army general's service cap, and so had gold cords and piping. Many photos show a woven Army eagle badge, but he also had an embroidered gold wire SS eagle, as here. The silver death's-head on the band is thus the only piece of regulation furniture on the cap.

The black Panzer vehicle uniform is, oddly but unmistakably, an early Army type with broad lapels and no collar-piping. Shoulder straps and collar patches of rank are conventional. Again, Dietrich was unique in wearing a non-regulation gold sleeve eagle and gold-embroidered 'Adolf Hitler' cuff title. The Crimea battle shield is worn on the sleeve above the eagle. On the left breast the decorations include an honorary award of the gold and diamond pilot/observer's badge; and his proudly-worn First World War tank crewman's battle badge, earned as a sergeant-major in the 13th (Bavarian) Tank Bn. in 1918, and one of less than 100 awarded. The gold Party Badge recalls his early enrolment in the NSDAP.

H1: Generaloberst Gotthard Heinrici, 1945
This too-often forgotten general commanded 4th Army before Moscow in early 1942, and Army Group Vistula in March–April 1945, until dismissed by Keitel over his refusal to commit his troops to suicidal defence of hopeless positions. He was a cousin of von Rundstedt; of the same unbending stock, and a devout Protestant, he spent part of the war in disgrace over his silent refusal to give up public church-going at Hitler's request. He was a master of the outnumbered defence. Photos show him in the 'old style' field cap and an issue-pattern reversible, camouflaged, padded winter combat jacket with a rank patch on the sleeve; he hated top-boots and habitually wore old First World War leather leggings with ankle-boots.

H2: Grossadmiral Karl Dönitz, 1944
The Navy service cap had a larger, less stiffened outline than those of the other services; of navy blue with a black ribbed band, it bore gold insignia for all officer ranks, and two rows of gold oakleaves on the cloth-faced peak for admirals. The double-breasted uniform tunic and straight trousers were worn over shoes. Ranking was displayed on the tunic shoulders and cuffs; the shoulder straps of this rank corresponded to those of GFM, but on blue backing. The admiral's greatcoat had bright blue lapel facings; note also the dress dagger, in Navy officer's pattern, suspended from fittings under the left pocket flap. The baton, its shaft covered in blue material, was generally similar to that of a marshal but featured a foul-anchor motif.

H3: SS-Gruppenführer Hermann Fegelein, 1945
Fegelein, as husband of the sister of Eva Braun, served out the last months of the war as Himmler's SS liaison officer at the Führerbunker. He was suspected of complicity with Himmler in un-

Dönitz with some of his U-boat commanders in May 1943, as C-in-C of the German Navy. By this date the tide was turning in favour of the Allies in the submarine war; March 1943 was the last really dangerous month, with 108 vessels totalling 627,000 tons sunk. In May 40 U-boats were destroyed at sea or in their pens; in July 37 were sunk, mostly by the growing Allied maritime air effort; and by the end of 1943 the Allies were losing only some 80,000 tons a month.

authorised contacts and attempted negotiations with the Allies, and late in April 1945 Hitler had him taken out and shot. We need not weep for him; as commander of the 8. SS-Kavallerie-Division 'Florian Geyer' on 'anti-partisan' operations behind the front lines in Russia in 1941–43 he had almost certainly been implicated in several disgusting atrocities. He wears a beautifully cut W-SS general's service uniform with white-striped riding breeches. Ranking at collar and shoulder is conventional. Among his decorations are the Close Combat Bar high on the left breast, and the War Order of the German Cross in Gold on the right breast. He retains his old divisional cuff title.

Notes sur les planches en couleur

A1: Une photo montre Guderian en uniforme de commandant de la 2. Panzer-Div., 1937. Les pattes d'épaule de grade sont portées sur la veste et la capote. **A2**: Uniforme règlementaire sauf le fond blanc des pattes d'épaules, la soutache blanche et l'insigne de col blanc et argent – tous indiquant la position de Chef du 18. Inf. Regt. **A3**: Tunique du général ornementée, avec soutache rouge. A l'époque la casquette de montagne manqua le passepoil du rang. Notez l'insigne de guide montagnard.

B1: Galland, à l'époque commandant du JG 26 sur les côtes de la Manche, portait parfois ces vêtements 'Irvin' capturés de la RAF. Le cigare était coutumier. **B2**: Le fameux commandant des Stukas porte la Fliegerbluse ornée d'un brassard Richthofen-Gerschwader de la guerre 1914–18. **B3**: Uniforme règlementaire du général de la Luftwaffe; les décorations comprennent le Krimschild et le brassard Kreta, ainsi que la version or et diamant de l'insigne de pilote, décerné par Göring en personne.

C1: Une photo en couleur prise en Tunisie montre cet uniforme plutôt que du modèle plus souvent illustré. Revers rouges de la capote tropicale marron. **C2**: En tant que chef d'état-major de Rommel, Bayerlein porte l'uniforme tropical d'un colonel de Panzertruppe. Beaucoup d'officiers ne prenaient pas la peine de changer les insignes de col et de poitrine des vestes règlementaires et gardaient le modèle des hommes de troupe, comme ici. **C3**: Notez les différences entre les uniformes tropicaux des armées de terre et de l'air; aussi, casquette de campagne 'Meyer' de la Luftwaffe en Mediterranée.

D1: Casquette d'été blanche au-dessus, des généraux de la Luftwaffe; et 'l'Interimstab', version ordinaire du bâton de maréchal. **D2**: Notez l'aigle épinglé sur la poitrine de cette tunique blanche. **D3**: L'uniforme que von Arnim portait lors de sa reddition en Tunisie. Les généraux avaient des uniformes tropicaux faits sur mesure en olive ou brun, avec la casquette 'feldgrau'. Les chaussettes longues sont une note personnelle. . . .

E1: Cordons et boutons ôtés du Schirmmütze, en campagne. **E2**: L'insigne sur les casquettes des généraux passa d'argent à or en janvier 1943; un ordre postérieur spécifiant l'utilisation de l'argent était souvent ignoré. Inhabituels, deux brassards sur la même manchette. **E3**: Manstein portait des uniformes très simples. Sur une photo plus tardive, il porte un tunique à col 'feldgrau' et une casquette à insigne d'or.

F1: Les pattes d'épaule sont à fond jaune-cavalerie et portent le '8' du régiment de cavalerie dont von Kleist était le commandant honoraire. Le col doublé de fourrure et la casquette de fourrure sont des additions personnelles typiques à l'uniforme de service en Russie. **F2**: Steiner porte la capote caoutchoutée de motocycliste avec col de tissu gris, variante populaire de la capote habituelle. **F3**: Beaucoup de généraux portaient une version à passepoil doré de la casquette de campagne de 1943. La veste de mouton, une acquisition personnelle, a sur la manche gauche la pièce indiquant le grade, qu'on mettait sur les vêtements de combat dénués de pattes d'épaules.

G1: La casquette porte un mélange d'insignes de l'armée et de SS. La veste camouflée est une affectation personnelle, avec pattes d'épaules rapportées. **G2**: Meindl porte une vieille blouse de parachutiste avec pièces de rang sur chaque manche; il a ajouté une jugulaire or à sa casquette, ce qui lui donne un air excentrique. Le petit insigne au côté de la casquette semble être celui de son unité, un 'M' ailé. **G3**: Uniforme hautement individuel à bords et insigne dorés à la place de l'argent règlementaire. Modèle de l'armée et non de SS. Les décorations comprennent l'insigne honoraire de pilote en or et diamant, et l'insigne d'équipage de tanks de 1918.

H1: L'obscur mais remarquable commandant du Groupe d'Armée Vistula en mars-avril 1945, avec une veste d'hiver règlementaire molletonnée, reversible et camouflée. Il portait toujours des jambières de cuir de la guerre 1914–18 à la place de bottes. **H2**: Notez le poignard de parade et bâton d'amiral. **H3**: Le 'beau-frère' d'Hitler servait comme officier de liaison d'Himmler dans le Führerbunker; Hitler le fit fusiller peu avant la fin de la guerre. Son uniforme du général de Waffen-SS a encore le brassard de division de son commandement précédent.

Farbtafeln

A1: Ein Foto zeigt ihn, diese Uniform als Kommandeur der 2. Panzerdivision im Jahre 1937 tragend. Die Schulterrangklappen wurden auf beiden, Jacke und Mantel, getragen. **A2**: Vorschriftsuniform, ausser dem weissen Untergrund an den Schulterklappen, der weissen Paspel und den silbernen und weissen Kragenabzeichen – alle diese markieren seinen Rang als Chef des 18. Inf.Regt. **A3**: Beachte die reich verzierte, rot paspelierte Version einer Generalsdienstjacke; das Fehlen der Paspel an dem Oberhauptssaum der Bergmütze zu dieser Zeit; sowie das Bergführerabzeichen.

B1: Galland, zu dieser Zeit Kommandeur der JG 26 an der Kanalküste, trug manchmal diese erbeutete RAF 'Irvin' Fliegerkleidung. Die Zigarre war üblich. **B2**: Der berühmte Stuka-Kommandeur trägt die Fliegerbluse mit den Ärmelstreifen des Richthofen-Geschwaders vom Ersten Weltkrieg geschmückt. **B3**: Luftwaffengenerals-Vorschriftsuniform; Auszeichnungen beinhalten die Krimschild und Kreta Ärmelstreifen und die goldene und diamantene Version des Pilotenabzeichens, von Göring persönlich verliehen.

C1: Ein Farbfoto, in Tunesien aufgenommen, zeigt diese Uniform anstelle der gewöhnlicherweise abgebildeten Version. Beachte die roten Aufschläge auf dem braunen tropischen Übermantel. **C2**: Fotografiert an Rommels Stabschef, trägt er die tropische Uniform eines Panzeroberst. Viele Offiziere hielten es nicht für nötig, die Kragen- und Brustabzeichen der ausgegebenen Jacken zu ändern und behielten, wie hier, das Muster des normalen Soldaten. **C3**: Beachte die Unterschiede zwischen der tropischen Uniform der Armee und der Luftwaffe; und 'Meyer' Feldmütze der Luftwaffe im Mittelmeerraum.

D1: Beachte die Sommermütze mit weissem Oberteil eines Luftwaffengenerals, und den Interimstab, die Alltagsdienstversion der Marschallstabes. **D2**: Bemerke das an der weissen Jacke getragene Adler-Brustansteckabzeichen. **D3**: Die Uniform, die er in Tunesien zur Kapitulation trug. Die Generäle trugen für individuell geschneiderte tropische Uniformen in braunen oder olivfarbenen Schattierungen, getragen mit der feldgrauen Schirmmütze. Die langen Socken sind eine persönliche Note!

E1: Bemerke, Kordeln und Knöpfe sind vor der Schirmmütze für den Gebrauch im Feld entfernt. **E2**: Das Abzeichen an der Generalsmütze wechselte im Januar 1943 von silber zu gold; ein späterer Befehl, der die Weiterbenutzung des silbernen anordnete, wurde oft nicht beachtet. Bemerke das ungewöhnliche Herzeigen zweier Ärmelstreifen am selben Aufschlag. **E3**: Manstein trug sehr einfache Uniformen. Ein späteres Foto zeigt ihn in einer Jacke mit feldgrauem Kragen und einer Schiffchenmütze mit goldenen Abzeichen.

F1: Die Schulterstreifen sind auf kavalleriegelbem Hintergrund und tragen die '8' des Kavallerieregiments, in dem er Ehrenkommandeur war. Der pelzbesetzte Kragen und Pelzmütze sind eine typische persönliche Beifügung der Uniform für den Dienst in Russland. **F2**: Steiner trägt den gummibeschichteten Mantel eines Motorradfahrers mit einem grauen Tuchkragen, eine beliebte Alternative zum Übermantel. **F3**: Viele Generäle trugen eine goldverzierte Version der 1943er Einheitsfeldmütze. Die persönlich angeschafte Schafpelzjacke trägt das linke Ärmelrangabzeichen wie es an der Kampfkleidung, die keine Schulterstreifen zeigte, getragen wurde.

G1: Die Einheitsfeldmütze trägt eine seltsame Abzeichensammlung, Armee und SS. Die Jacke aus Tarnungsmaterial ist eine persönliche Affektiertheit – beachte die beigefügten Schulterstreifen. **G2**: Meindl trägt einen alten Fallschirmjägerkittel mit Rangabzeichen an beiden Ärmeln; und hat goldene Kinnkordeln zu seiner Einheitsfeldmütze hinzugefügt, was ihm eine exzentrische Erscheinung gibt. Das kleine Abzeichen auf der Seite seiner Mütze scheint das seiner Einheit zu sein, ein geflügeltes 'M'. **G3**: Eine höchstpersönliche Uniform mit goldenen Verzierungen und Abzeichen anstelle der angeordneten silbernen an verschiedenen Stellen. Bemerke, dass sie nach Armee- und nicht SS-Muster ist. Auszeichnungen schliessen ein Ehrenabzeichen des goldenen und diamantenen Pilotenabzeichens ein; sowie das 1918er Panzermannschaftsabzeichen.

H1: Der unbekannte, jedoch hervorragende Kommandeur der Armeegruppe Vistula im März-April 1945 trägt eine nach Vorschriftsausgabe wattierte, auf beiden Seiten tragbare, getarnte Winterjacke. Er trug immer Ledergamaschen aus dem Ersten Weltkrieg anstelle von hohen Stiefeln. **H2**: Beachte den Paradedolch und den Rangstab. **H3**: Hitlers 'Schwager' diente als Himmlers Verbindungsoffizier im Führerbunker; Hitler liess ihn ein paar Tage vor Kriegsende erschiessen. Seine Waffen-SS Generalsuniform behält den Ärmelstreifen der Division, die er zuvor kommandiert hat.